THE 8-WEEK CHOLESTEROL CURE COOKBOOK

Also by Robert E. Kowalski

THE 8-WEEK CHOLESTEROL CURE
CHOLESTEROL & CHILDREN

THE 8-WEEK CHOLESTEROL CURE COOKBOOK

More than 200 delicious recipes featuring the foods that have been proved to lower cholesterol

Robert E. Kowalski

THORSONS PUBLISHING GROUP

First published 1989 in the USA by Harper & Row, Publishers, Inc.,
10 East 53rd Street, New York, NY 10022

First UK edition, 1990

British Library Cataloguing in Publication Data

Kowalski, Robert E.
  The 8-week cholesterol cure cookbook.
  1. Food. Low cholesterol dishes. Recipes
  I. Title
  641.563

ISBN 0-7225-2231-2

*Published by Thorsons Publishing Group, Wellingborough,
Northamptonshire NN8 2RQ, England*

Typeset by Harper Phototypesetters Limited, Northampton, England
Printed and bound by HarperCollins Manufacturing, Glasgow

10 9 8 7 6 5 4 3 2

I dedicate this book to my mother, Helen, who encouraged my interest in cooking when I was just a child. She put up with me in the kitchen when I was more hindrance than help. An essential ingredient for any recipe is love, and there was plenty of that in our house throughout my childhood.

CONTENTS

ACKNOWLEDGEMENTS

The recipe for preparing this book calls for a generous mixing of the talents of many people. My thanks as always to my agent, Clyde Taylor, who guided the project along from the beginning. To Michele Urvater, for her culinary skills in recipe development. To my U.S. editors, Larry Ashmead and Margaret Wimberger; Margaret showed extraordinary patience on this one. And to Jennifer Jensen, R.D., for her able assistance and patience in doing the nutritional analyses of the recipes.

PART ONE

INTRODUCTION: DECLARING WAR ON CHOLESTEROL

Welcome to a most unusual cookbook, one that quite literally could help save your life. This is not another low-fat, low-calorie cookbook. For sure the world has enough of those, and many of them are quite good. Each of the recipes in this book contains foods that have the ability to actually lower your cholesterol level and to protect you from heart disease. And, if that isn't enough to entice you, eating these special foods will help you to maintain your weight, or even to lose a few pounds if necessary.

In the past we have heard only negatives when it came to following a heart-healthy diet. Don't eat this. Avoid that. The advice from well-meaning dietitians seemed to be, if a food tastes good, spit it out since it can't be good for you.

But what we've been learning in the past few years is that what you do eat is as important as what you avoid when it comes to protecting yourself from heart disease. A lot of what was accepted as gospel truth not long ago has been shown now to be incorrect. For example, even though salmon is a very fatty fish, it's actually a wise choice for a heart-healthy diet. If you've been avoiding such shellfish delicacies as oysters and scallops because you think they have too much cholesterol, you can now think again. You might equate red meat with heart attacks, but now I can show you how to enjoy red meat every week without putting yourself at risk. I'll teach you how to prepare recipes that will make your mouth water and your cholesterol drop.

In case you are not familiar with *The 8-Week Cholesterol Cure*, here is a brief introduction to my history with cholesterol and heart disease.

Even though I had been writing about health and medical issues for more than 20 years, cholesterol and heart disease remained just one more area of research to me until it became a matter of life and death. First, I had a family history of heart disease, having lost my dad to a massive heart attack when he was just 57 years old. Others in my family were also afflicted. Even then, I was not prepared for the heart attack that struck when I was only 35 years old. By the age of 41, I had undergone two coronary bypass surgeries. After the second one, I knew cholesterol was the culprit and something had to be done about it.

Unsatisfied by the options of either cholesterol-reducing drugs or a severely restricted diet, I turned to the medical literature for clues to another approach. Trained in both journalism and medical physiology, I had easy access to all that had been written about cholesterol and heart disease.

To save my own life, I developed what is now known as 'The 8-Week Cholesterol Cure'. It worked for me by lowering my cholesterol from a dangerous high 7.3 mmol/l down to a safe 4.3 mmol/l, without drugs and without deprivation. And it has worked for thousands of others who have read the book and followed my programme. At the core of my programme are foods and vitamins that I learned can dramatically lower cholesterol levels.

Today cholesterol is a household word. Just a few years ago, most of us couldn't even pronounce it, and many wondered whether all the fuss about it wasn't much ado about nothing. That all changed in August 1987, when in America the National Cholesterol Education Panel, a prestigious group of experts representing the American National Institutes of Health and 20 of America's top medical organizations, including the American Heart Association and the American Medical Association, reported that cholesterol levels for all men and women, regardless of age, should be no higher than 5.2 mmol/l.

The National Cholesterol Education Program has subsequently spread the word to both the public and doctors that everyone should have a cholesterol test, everyone should know his or her numbers, and if those levels are too high, something should be done about it.

We all have good reason for concern. Nearly 2 million Britons a year suffer from some form of heart disease and each year as many as 180,000 die from heart attacks in the U.K. Heart disease remains Britain's main cause of illness and premature death. It is the cause of one in three of all deaths among 55-64 year olds.

But there is good news, too. Heart disease is, to a large extent, a preventable disorder. We can accurately predict just who will perish, based on their risk factors. Certain factors cannot be altered: family history of heart disease, advanced age, and male sex all put one at undeniable risk. But we can most definitely control the other factors: high cholesterol levels, high blood pressure, and cigarette smoking are the 'Big Three' that can be changed. And we can also take charge of contributing factors, including a sedentary lifestyle, Type A behaviour patterns (marked especially by anger and hostility), obesity, and, to a very large extent, diabetes.

While all these risk factors contribute significantly to heart-disease mortality, the focus today remains on cholesterol. We have proof positive that reducing cholesterol levels can slash heart-attack and death rates. *For every 1 per cent cut in cholesterol, we achieve a 2 per cent drop in heart-disease risk.*

Many authorities believe that, while a cholesterol level of 5.2 mmol/l is a good start, we should shoot for even lower numbers. Dr William Castelli, director of the famed Framingham Heart Study, has stated that he has never seen a heart attack in a person whose cholesterol level was under 4 mmol/l. One of the pioneers in establishing the link between cholesterol and heart disease, Dr Jeremiah Stamler of Northwestern University, in Evanston, Illinois, U.S.A., maintains that between 4.1 and 4.6 mmol/l there is little if any risk of heart disease, but that after 4.6 the risk increases gradually, and that after 5.2 the risk goes up significantly. Moreover, if one looks at the incidence of heart disease in populations around the world, one finds that the lower the cholesterol levels, the lower the heart-disease rates.

Another reason for wanting to get cholesterol levels as low as possible comes from research into the potential for reversing heart disease. Investigators have found that only when cholesterol counts drop to the 4.1 level or below can one expect either to stop the progress of the disease or actually to reverse it.

We also have to consider the different kinds of cholesterol in our blood. A finger-prick test, such as is now available in many major health food stores and pharmacies gives a count of total blood cholesterol. A more thorough analysis, which can be done in hospital or clinical laboratories, reveals the amounts of the different kinds of cholesterol.

These types are based on the size and density of the chemical carriers, known as lipoproteins, that move cholesterol through the bloodstream to and from the liver where it is produced. Low-density-lipoprotein (LDL) cholesterol has been termed 'bad' cholesterol because this is the type that is deposited in arteries,

resulting in heart disease. High-density-lipoprotein (HDL) cholesterol, on the other hand, has been called 'good' cholesterol
because it is carried away from the artery walls and back to the
liver for disposal. We want to keep LDLs down and HDLs up.

How do we accomplish these goals? Official recommendations
in the U.K. are that you should derive no more than 35 per cent
of your energy (calories) as fat. (The average Briton currently
consumes 42 per cent of calories as fat.) That's excellent advice for
the general population, but for those with already elevated cholesterol levels this recommendation alone isn't enough. If one
starts out with a cholesterol level of 7, for example, a 10 per cent
reduction brings the individual down to 6, leaving him or her still
at risk. Even squeezing a bit more fat from the diet will not likely
bring the count to under 5.2, where it belongs.

On the other hand, severely restricted diets such as that
proposed in the Pritikin Programme can achieve remarkable
cholesterol reductions. But there are problems with these plans.
Reducing fat intake to the recommended 7 to 10 per cent of total
intake, especially for a lifetime, is difficult if not impossible for
most men and women. Few of us are willing to give up all our
favourite foods for the rest of our lives. This just isn't a practical
approach. Moreover, extremely low-fat diets reduce the levels not
only of the bad LDL cholesterol but of the good HDL cholesterol
as well.

Authorities advocate drugs if diet alone cannot reduce cholesterol levels sufficiently. Two such drugs, colestipol and cholestyramine, are called bile-sequestering agents because they grab onto
the bile acids in the intestine and prevent them from being
reabsorbed into the bloodstream by carrying them out of the body
in the bowel movement. Since bile acids are made from cholesterol, the body must draw some cholesterol out of the blood in
order to make more of those acids, which are needed in digestion.
Over time the cholesterol levels in the blood drop.

But cholesterol-lowering drugs are expensive and must be taken
for a lifetime. They are also extremely unpleasant to swallow, and
can cause some adverse reactions.

Imagine my dilemma, then, when faced with the urgent need
to reduce my own cholesterol level. Then imagine my delight at
finding that certain foods actually lower the amount of cholesterol
in the blood in exactly the same way as the drugs. Those foods,
including oat bran and oatmeal, dried beans and peas, barley,
certain fruits and vegetables, and rice bran, all contain soluble

fibre, which, like the drugs, binds onto bile acids in the digestive tract and literally carries the cholesterol right out of the body. We'll be discussing these foods in detail in this book.

But, whatever the benefits of these foods, most people aren't very familiar with cooking dried beans and peas, or rice bran, or barley. In fact, when I first wrote *The 8-Week Cholesterol Cure*, very few had even heard of oat bran, much less rice bran. I included some recipes in that book, but a gap remained. I realized that people need to learn a lot more about those cholesterol-lowering foods and how they can be used on a daily basis. And, even though I've been cooking as a hobby since I was just 13 years old, I too wanted to learn more about cooking with those foods.

I was delighted, then, to be introduced to Michele Urvater by my editor at Harper & Row, Margaret Wimberger.

Michele began her cooking career as a chef in the New York restaurant Ruskay's. In 1976 she established her own cooking school, listed in the *New York Times* as 'one of the premier schools in the city'. Since closing the school in 1981, Michele has been involved in virtually all aspects of professional cooking and is today a cooking consultant and frequent contributor to food magazines.

It turned out that Michele was very much interested in working with me to develop some new recipes for a book that would focus exclusively on those foods which have been proved to reduce cholesterol and to protect against heart disease.

After a handshake by telephone, I started to make a 'wish list' of all the ways I wanted to cook and bake with those wonderful foods. I suggested to Michele, for example, that guacamole was delicious but high in fat; could she, I wondered, come up with an alternative recipe made with beans and peas? As you'll soon see, she did that and far more.

Whilst Michele was sweating over her stove, I experimented with recipes at home. After four and a half years, I was hungry for some new oat-bran muffin recipes. And I was finding all sorts of new food products and equipment that offered lots of promise. Between the two of us, we came up with more than 200 recipes designed to keep the heart healthy, the stomach content, and the mouth watering. These recipes are designed to fit into my total programme for cholesterol reduction. Pick one of the recipes to start with today. Bon appétit!

A DIET TO LIVE WITH FOR LIFE

Any successful programme to reduce cholesterol must have a good, low-fat, low-cholesterol diet as its foundation. But you can enjoy a wide variety of all kinds of foods and still achieve tremendous success. Importantly, you won't have to eliminate certain types of foods totally, as you do with some fad diets that no one can stay with for long. In fact, you'll probably find that eating the way I propose will keep you more satisfied than your present diet.

The food we eat must provide the nutrients we need for energy, performance of bodily functions, and maintenance and repair. But keeping track of individual nutrients can be confusing. Do you have any idea how much selenium you had today? Or the amount of copper and zinc in last week's menus? No one does, yet it is important that we get enough of those trace minerals, along with the more recognized nutrients such as calcium, protein, and iron.

Recognizing that people couldn't possibly keep track of the many individual nutrients, nutritionists long ago developed an approach that, with modifications, makes as much sense today as it did 60 years ago. This approach is based on the four food groups: meats, fish, and meat alternatives; milk and other dairy foods; fruits and vegetables; and breads and cereals. In addition, we can include a fifth group of other foods that supply little if any nutrition but do provide food satisfaction. Each of these categories of foods tends to supply a group of major nutrients not readily available in any of the other categories. And, when foods from all the groups are consumed on a regular basis, one can be certain of getting enough of both the major and minor nutrients.

The first group is better named the 'protein group'. It includes meat, fish and seafood, poultry, eggs, and other meat alternatives. Any or all of these will provide protein needed for maintenance and repair of the body. Adults need two servings a day, with a serving of meat measured as 3½ ounces to satisfy the daily protein requirements. Of course, protein foods supply a number of other nutrients as well.

In selecting foods from the meat group, those conscious of cholesterol will opt for lean cuts of beef, the white meat of poultry, lots of fish and seafood, egg whites, and other meat alternatives. Happily, the meat alternatives are some of the same foods that also lower cholesterol, as we'll see in detail later in this book—dried beans and peas, lentils, split yellow and green peas, chick-peas, and so forth. I'll show you how they can be used in entrées, soups, salads, and dips.

The second group is typically a major contributor of fat and cholesterol in the diet, which is notorious for its high fat content. These are dairy products, which are the main supplier of calcium in the diet, as well as providing substantial protein and a variety of other nutrients. While we never outgrow our need for milk and other dairy foods, we never need the excessive fat and cholesterol that comes along with many of them.

Picking foods from this group means opting for the low-fat varieties. Start looking at the fat listings on dairy foods to pick those with the least fat. Today you can easily find low-fat yogurt, very-low-fat cottage cheese, and reduced-fat cheeses.

Fat presents virtually no problem for the next food group, the fruits and vegetables. Generally speaking, fruits provide the best source of vitamin C, while vegetables supply abundant vitamin A. Adults need at least two servings of fruit each day, and at least two servings of vegetables. The emphasis here is on *at least*; when you cut back on fat, you can enjoy far more food, and fruits and vegetables really fill the bill.

For the most part you can eat fruits and vegetables with no worry about fat. And of course there is no cholesterol since that comes only from animal sources. The only fruits to be somewhat wary of are olives and avocados, which contain a lot of fat and so should be eaten in moderation.

Every mother tells her children: 'Eat your vegetables, they're good for you!' Of course we always knew that Mum was right, but now we're learning that she was absolutely on target when it comes to preventing heart disease. Three major recent American studies zeroing in on vegetables were reported at the First International Congress on Vegetarian Nutrition held in Washington DC in 1987.

Dr Michael Burr reported on a study that compared vegetarian and non-vegetarian customers of health-food stores. As they were health-food store shoppers, it was assumed that both groups would share an interest in healthful eating habits. A total of nearly 11,000 men and women were followed for 10 to 12 years.

Death rates from heart disease were significantly lower in the vegetarians than in the non-vegetarians, especially among men. Cholesterol levels were lower in vegetarians, but not tremendously so, and there was no difference in blood pressure readings. Dr Burr concluded that vegetarianism seems to confer some protection against heart disease, but he remains inconclusive as to 'whether this is due to abstinence from meat or to a high consumption of vegetables'.

Several studies have shown that Seventh Day Adventists, who avoid meat of all kinds, have a lower rate of heart disease than non-Adventists. Dr Gary Fraser of Loma Linda University, in California, reported his long-term data at the Congress, showing that, indeed, vegetarian Adventists enjoy protection from heart attacks.

In discussing his findings, Dr Fraser said the lower risk in Adventist men could be owing to their dietary habits, non-smoking status, possibly better exercise habits, and greater social support. Or could it be the religious practices of the Adventists that protected them, in terms of a sense of community or reduction of stress?

Dr V. Fonnebo looked at those possibilities with groups of Adventists in Norway. His Tromso Heart Study has become a classic in the field of nutrition and health. To examine the potential role of religion in conferring protection against heart disease, Dr Fonnebo compared Adventists with equally fervent Baptists. When all other risk factors were taken into consideration, the serum cholesterol levels of the Adventists appeared to be the only factor protecting them from death by heart attack. Dr Fonnebo concluded that religion is not a factor.

Now you might conclude that it's a simple matter of avoiding saturated fat and cholesterol in the diet of the Adventists. But in fact the Adventists are lacto-ovo vegetarians, consuming quite large quantities of dairy foods and eggs. In some cases, the saturated fat and cholesterol contents of their diets are higher than those in meat eaters. But there remains a big difference in the amount of fruit and vegetables consumed regularly.

No one has the final answer yet, and there may be a number of factors involved. And even the leaders within the Adventist church are trying to persuade their members to cut back significantly on the amount of dairy foods and eggs they consume, regardless of other dietary practices. So don't assume that eating more fruits and vegetables will give you *carte blanche* to eat all the cheese and butter you want.

But the fact remains that something in the fruits and vegetables does indeed offer some protection against heart disease as well as against other diseases such as cancer. If nothing else, the more fruits and vegetables you eat, the less saturated fat and cholesterol are likely to be in your diet. An apple is a far better snack than a doughnut. And an extra-large salad or serving of vegetables at dinner will help cut back on the serving size of meat on the plate.

I'm far from a vegetarian. In fact, I believe that man was meant to be an omnivore, a creature who eats a little of this and a little of that rather than a meat-eating carnivore or a plant-eating herbivore. It's a question of balance. And certainly we've seen the specific benefits in terms of certain seafood rich in the oils which offer protection to the Eskimos. Many of the meat, fish, and poultry choices available supply us with high-quality protein with far less saturated fat and cholesterol than cheese and eggs. However, I do believe that everyone interested in total health—not just heart disease—ought to eat lots more fruit and vegetables. There's absolutely no down side to eating fruits and vegetables.

All types of fruits and vegetables contain *insoluble* fibre. That fibre, not the soluble type, moves food more quickly through the digestive tract. The short-term benefit is greater bowel movement regularity. The long-term benefit appears to be protection from diseases of the colon such as cancer.

In addition, many kinds of fruits and vegetables are rich in soluble fibre. Take a look at the numbers in the table on page 43. I hasten to point out that we currently have no clinical evidence that the soluble fibre in those foods will directly lower cholesterol levels, however. Until studies are done with human subjects we won't know for sure whether that particular source of soluble fibre is as effective as, say, oat bran or dried beans and peas.

To be effective in jacking up your fruit and vegetable consumption, as well as that of your family, try to be a bit creative. A bowl of limp lettuce leaves with a chunk of tomato doesn't make anyone look forward to the next salad. Go for all the variety you can think of: different kinds of lettuce, grated carrots, little florets of cauliflower and broccoli, artichoke hearts, raisins, palm hearts, and so on.

Keep some prepared fruits and vegetables in the refrigerator in bowls or sealed containers so you can get them easily. No one wants to start peeling and paring at 10 p.m. for that little snack. Make it convenient.

Finally we come to the breads and cereals group, sometimes called the grain group. Here's where we'll find a lot of beneficial dietary fibre, both soluble and insoluble, along with a wealth of B vitamins. Adults need a minimum of four servings daily. Again, those on low-fat diets will find they can eat a lot more from this group without worrying about weight gain. I delight in amazing my friends with the amounts of pasta I can put away at one sitting, or to finish a big meal and then ask for another basket of bread and rolls. Of course I don't put butter on that bread, so I can eat a lot more.

Baked goods and some cereals, however, can be a significant source of hidden fat in the diet. You'll have to start reading the labels carefully to learn just what you're buying. One brand of rolls, for example, will be made with a bit of corn or soybean oil while another uses animal shortening. No need to tell you which to choose. The same applies to breakfast cereals. It really disturbs me that some manufacturers will make oat-bran cereals with coconut oil, which is a far more saturated form of fat than even lard or butter.

While the foods in those four basic food groups provide all the nutrients we need, other foods supply a lot of calories along with their taste appeal. Those 'others', including fats and oils, sugars, alcohol, and salt form a fifth group. We know from a great number of authorities that we should all eat a lot less of those foods.

First let's consider fats and oils. Recipes taste a whole lot better with them than without them. So the key here must be moderation. Choosing fats and oils to cook and bake with can be difficult, and nutrition labels can be confusing. So let's take a closer look, beginning with a bit of basic chemistry.

All fats and oil are composed of varying combinations of individual molecules termed fatty acids. Depending on the composition of those molecules, the fats are termed saturated, monounsaturated, or polyunsaturated. By now you've most likely heard that saturated fats are responsible for raising blood cholesterol and for clogging of the arteries, while polyunsaturated and monounsaturated fats are not. In fact, when poly- and monounsaturated fats are used to replace saturated fats in the diet, cholesterol levels fall.

Just a few years ago authorities recommended polyunsaturated fats such as corn and soybean oil, viewing the monounsaturated fats as 'neutral', neither raising nor lowering cholesterol levels. But today we know that both are efficient in reducing cholesterol counts, but that monounsaturated fats do a better job of protecting levels of the good cholesterol, the HDLs. Too much polyunsaturated fat can decrease the HDLs along with the LDLs.

All *fats* contain saturated, polyunsaturated, and monounsaturated fatty acids. But different foods have different fatty-acid profiles, with one kind of fatty acids predominant. That's why we use a kind of shorthand to describe foods as being saturated, polyunsaturated, or monounsaturated. We can simplify things further by generalizing that animal fats are principally sources of saturated fats. Vegetable oils, on the other hand, are mainly unsaturated or monounsaturated. But, of course, there are exceptions: the tropical oils, including coconut oil, palm oil, and palm kernel oil, are mainly saturated fats.

Saturated fats are solid to semi-solid at room temperature, while the polyunsaturated and monounsaturated fats are liquid at that temperature. But some polyunsaturated fats can be hardened through the process of hydrogenation. By hydrogenating such oils as corn and soybean, food manufacturers extend shelf-life and make products more appealing in taste and texture. In the past we have been told to avoid or at least limit hydrogenated or partially hydrogenated fats, since they have been made more saturated, but fortunately we've learned some facts that have changed that.

Working at the University of Texas Health Sciences Center in Dallas, Dr Scott Grundy compared the effects of isolated specific fatty acids on cholesterol levels in the blood. He fed volunteers diets that contained one of three fatty acids. When effects of the saturated fats stearic acid and palmitic acid were compared with those of the polyunsaturated fat oleic acid, only the palmitic acid raised cholesterol levels. The process of hydrogenating polyunsaturated fats for such products as margarine creates stearic acid. So, while the products' fats are more saturated, we now know that the specific fatty acid, stearic, isn't a concern. So we can choose products containing hydrogenated fats, watching only that we limit the total amount of fat in the diet. We'll look at that limitation in just a little while.*

---

* Early reports of Dr Grundy's work misinterpreted the data. Since beef and chocolate contain stearic acid, some said this made these foods OK! They overlooked the fact that those foods also contain palmitic acid.

Dr Grundy was the man who also brought the monounsaturated fats to the public attention. He and others had long noted that Italians, Greeks, and others of Mediterranean descent were largely protected from heart disease even though their diets were high in total fat. Dr Grundy wondered whether it might have something to do with the olive oil they were consuming. He was right. Olive oil, rich in monounsaturated fatty acids, was able to lower cholesterol as efficiently as polyunsaturated fats when used to replace saturated fats in the diet. Moreover, the monounsaturated fats did not lower HDL levels, thus making them superior to the polyunsaturated fats.

The recommendation today is strictly to limit saturated fats, replacing them with monounsaturated and some polyunsaturated fats. Here are the sources of those fats in the diet:

SATURATED FATS: Animal fats in meat, dairy products, and animal shortenings. Tropical oils, including coconut, palm, and palm kernel oils

MONOUNSATURATED FATS: Olives and olive oil, peanuts and peanut oil, avocados, cashews

POLYUNSATURATED FATS: Vegetable oils, including corn oil, soybean oil, safflower oil, and others

For a complete breakdown of the percentages of saturated, monounsaturated, and polyunsaturated fatty acids in commonly consumed fats and oils, see the table on page 24. But as you limit total fat intake and replace saturates with unsaturates, how much is enough and how much is too much?

The average Briton consumes 42 per cent of his or her calories as fat. The U.K. Committee on Medical Aspects of Food Policy (COMA) says that number should be reduced to no more than 35 per cent for the entire population. Nathan Pritikin felt that one needed to go down to 7-10 per cent in order to achieve significant cholesterol lowering. I believe that one can succeed with a compromise level of fat intake and still reduce cholesterol significantly because of the other foods that can bring the counts down. From my own experience and from that of thousands of others who have had success with my programme, I find that a 20 per cent fat intake allows one to see a dramatic cholesterol drop and still fully enjoy foods at home and away, and to live without a feeling of deprivation.

But most people's eyes just glaze over at the thought of

Comparison of Dietary Fats and Oils

Type	Saturated Fatty Acids (% of Total)*	Monounsaturated Fatty Acids (% of Total)*	Polyunsaturated Fatty Acids (% of Total)*
Walnut oil	9	23	64
Safflower oil	10	13	77
Sunflower oil	11	20	69
Corn oil	13	25	62
Olive oil	14	77	9
Soybean oil	15	24	61
Peanut oil	18	49	33
Margarine (tub)	18	47	31
Chicken fat	30	45	11
Margarine	31	47	22
Lard	40	45	11
Mutton fat	47	41	8
Palm oil	49	37	9
Beef fat	50	42	4
Butterfat	62	29	4
Palm kernel oil	81	11	2
Coconut oil	86	6	2

*Percentages are averaged and thus may not total exactly 100 per cent.

calculating percentages. What do those percentages really mean in terms of what we eat? How can we really know what percentage of fat is being consumed? Not all foods have fat percentages printed on their labels, and even if we do know the specific percentage of fat for a specific food, how does that relate to the day's total? Fortunately, there is a practical, usable approach to monitoring fat intake.

If you look at the labels on foods, you'll see fat listed in grams per serving. That's pretty straightforward. But now how can one determine how many grams of fat should be in the daily diet? And will that number be the same for everyone? Here is a way to determine your personal prescription for daily fat intake.

As you know, you need a certain number of calories each day in order to maintain bodily functions and for energy. The more active you are physically, the more calories you need. Men typically burn more calories than women do, because they have greater muscle mass, and it is muscle that burns the calories. And, to a lesser degree, the need for calories diminishes as we get older.

A moderately active male needs about 15 calories per pound to maintain weight. More than that and he will gain weight, less and he'll lose. If he's a bit more active, he may need 16 calories per pound; a bit less active, and the calorie requirement drops. Women, on average, need a calorie or two less than men in each category of age and activity.

For a specific example, let's look at a moderately active male of middle age. Our sample specimen weighs 150 pounds (10½ stones/70 kg) to match his 5-foot-10-inch frame. Or he *wants* to weigh 150 pounds in which case he should feed only the pounds he wants, and the excess weight will gradually disappear. So he'll need 15 calories to maintain each of those 150 pounds. Let's do the mathematics:

$$\text{150 pounds} \times \text{15 calories} = \text{2250 calories per day}$$

Of those 2250 calories we want our man to have 20 per cent as fat. That bit of maths is just as simple:

$$\text{2250 calories} \times .20 = \text{450 calories as fat}$$

But how do we get from calories to grams of fat? One gram of protein or carbohydrate yields 4 calories. One gram of fat yields 9 calories. Therefore, 450 calories will come from 50 grams of fat, as determined in this simple calculation:

$$\text{450 calories} \div \text{9 calories per gram} = \text{50 grams}$$

Now we know our male example will be allowed a total of 50 grams of fat daily. He can count those grams easily by just looking at food nutrition labels, by learning a bit about the amount of fat contained in some commonly consumed foods.

Now it's time to plug your own numbers into the equations to determine your optimal fat intake as measured in grams.

$$\underset{ideal\ weight}{\underline{\qquad\qquad}} \times \underset{calories\ per\ pound}{\underline{\qquad\qquad}} = \text{daily calories}$$

$$\underset{daily\ calories}{\underline{\qquad\qquad}} \times .20 = \text{daily calories as fat}$$

$$\underset{daily\ calories\ as\ fat}{\underline{\qquad\qquad}} \div 9 = \text{daily grams of fat}$$

It is recommended that, of the total amount of fat you eat, no more than one-third should come from saturated fats. Similarly, less than one-third should come from polyunsaturated fats. The balance of fat calories should be provided by monounsaturated fats.

It's impractical to calculate fat intake to such an extent. Moreover, you don't always know the fatty-acid profile of a given food. But by adhering to a few practical guidelines you will come very close to achieving the recommendation.

First, limit your consumption of meat to two servings daily, with a serving being no more than 5 ounces, and usually about 3½ ounces. (The reason for that discrepancy is that servings in restaurants tend to be larger, and you'll want slightly larger servings at dinner, while you can feel very satisfied with a 3½-ounce serving at lunch or breakfast.) Of course there are some foods in this category that have very few grams of fat per serving, and you'll be able to enjoy larger servings of these more often.

You'll want to avoid completely many of the prime sources of saturated fat. Butter, lard, whole milk, high-fat cheeses, and premium ice creams have no place in a cholesterol-fighting programme. The same applies to tropical oils; read labels carefully in order to keep them out of your shopping bag.

Second, use cooking oils known to be high in monounsaturated fats rather than polyunsaturated fats. Those include olive oil. If there are certain recipes you have which you feel simply work better with corn or safflower oil, that's fine.

Polyunsaturated fats will come from a variety of foods, including breads and rolls made with corn or soybean oil. You'll also get polyunsaturated fats in margarine. I prefer the calorie-reduced margarines.

But what about dietary cholesterol?

By now you've probably noticed that I haven't even mentioned cholesterol in the diet. Many years ago nutritionists and dietitians saw that limiting dieters' cholesterol had little impact on reducing cholesterol levels in the blood. In fact, that kind of research fuelled the fires of controversy for years. It was only later that we realized that fat, especially saturated fat, had more influence than dietary cholesterol itself on blood cholesterol levels. So merely limiting cholesterol in the diet isn't enough; you must also cut back on total fat and saturated fat. However, that doesn't mean you can completely ignore the cholesterol in foods.

Actually, when you're watching out for saturated fats, the cholesterol pretty much watches out for itself. Only animal foods supply cholesterol. As you cut back on those animal foods, especially as you proceed from whole-milk dairy foods to the low-fat and nonfat varieties, you automatically cut back on cholesterol.

In the U.S. the American Heart Association calls for no more than 100 milligrams of cholesterol daily for each 1000 calories consumed. For a person consuming 2250 calories, as in our earlier example, total cholesterol intake should not exceed 225 milligrams. And, the AHA says, no one should eat more than 300 milligrams, regardless of the calories consumed.

Looking at the numbers in the table on page 24 you'll see that it won't be difficult at all to stay within those limits just by limiting your total fat consumption. You'll also notice that all meats—beef, chicken, turkey, fish, shellfish—have cholesterol. And most of those meats have equivalent amounts. Therefore, there's little point in choosing your meat on the basis of cholesterol content; choose rather by the amount of fat. That principle even applies to shellfish, which, as you'll observe, have more cholesterol than most meats.

There has been a great deal of confusion about shellfish. In the past, dietitians recommended not eating them because the cholesterol content was thought to be astronomically high. But those early testing methods were in error. Cholesterol is a sterol, and chemically related to the neutral sterols in plants. Testing devices at the time of those early tests couldn't tell the difference between sterols from animals—cholesterol—and sterols from plants, which do not affect cholesterol levels in the blood. We now know that shellfish have perhaps half the cholesterol listed in early charts; the plants they eat affect the readings.

Moreover, the fat content of shellfish is infinitesimal. Even if a portion of shellfish contains 100 milligrams of cholesterol, you can easily work that into the day's total. Dr William Castelli, of Framingham Heart Study fame, says if you can't be a vegetarian, eat a vegetarian of the sea. He believes that even shrimp, one of the highest in cholesterol of all shellfish, is as acceptable as chicken breast.

At first, keeping track of the grams of fat in foods will be demanding. But as with any new skill, you'll get better and better at it, until one day you realize you pay little or no attention to individual numbers and yet you're well within your limits. The quicker you learn where the fat is, and how to get rid of it, the easier it will be.

If you are not already used to keeping track of the fat in the food you eat, here's the best way to start. On your next three trips to the supermarket, allow yourself an extra 20 minutes. Use that time to read labels. You'll quickly see that what the manufacturer wants you to see may not be what you need to know about the food you're thinking about buying. For example, does the box of biscuits proudly proclaim on the front of the package that the food is 'cholesterol free . . . made only with vegetable oil'? Read the nutrition label and you just might see that the vegetable oil in question is coconut, palm, or palm kernel oil, which we've learned are responsible for raising blood cholesterol.

After three such shopping-reading trips, you'll have a pretty good idea as to what products are best for you and your family. By the third or fourth grocery run, you'll be repeating foods you frequently use, and you won't need to read those labels any longer.

Happily, a number of food manufacturers have begun to recognize that consumers want healthful foods and have started to remove some of the offending ingredients, such as animal fat and tropical oils. You'll want to keep an eye out for such changes.

Nutrition labels appear on most processed foods and on any food that makes a nutritional claim, such as 'low-fat' or 'reduced calorie'. So you can expect to see labels on almost all foods, with the exceptions of fresh meats, fruits and vegetables, and fresh bakery goods. Labelling is in two parts, the first giving the nutrition content of the food per serving. The serving size will be stated, along with the number of servings in the package. As an example, you'll see a breakdown of calories, protein, carbohydrates, fat, cholesterol, sodium, and potassium per serving, in grams and milligrams. Next you'll read the percentage of the Recommended Daily Amounts for some or all of the following nutrients: protein, vitamin A, vitamin C, thiamine, riboflavin, niacin, calcium, iron, vitamin D, vitamin B_6, folic acid, vitamin B_{12}, phosphorus, magnesium, zinc, and pantothenic acid.

Finally, you'll come to an ingredients listing at the bottom of the panel. Ingredients are listed in descending order according to weight. Thus, even though reduced-calorie margarine provides 100 per cent of its calories as fat, the first ingredient shown may be water if, in fact, there is more water in the product than oil. You'll also want to know just how much sugar might be lurking in a breakfast cereal. That's a bit more tricky, since sugars can be listed separately; you may well see four or five different kinds of sugar on one label. This allows the manufacturer to list flour or cereal as the principal ingredient, even though there's more sugar in the food than flour or cereal.

Ultimately, the responsibility for ensuring the quality of what gets from the supermarket shelf to your home resides with you. You have decisions to make with every purchase. Make those heart-healthy choices on the basis of the information you can glean from the nutrition labels on foods and on your increasing knowledge about foods in general. Obviously it's worth the effort, and that effort gets easier with each shopping trip.

Thus far we've discussed the role of the four basic food groups in nutrition, and fats and oils as two of the 'other' foods that don't quite fit into the food groups. I also mentioned sucrose and other sugars as I explained the meanings of food claims, pointing out that, in moderation, sugar poses no health problems.

Next we come to alcohol. I'm happy to report that virtually every study done has shown that those who enjoy a drink on a fairly regular basis live longer than those who abstain from alcohol. Of course the watchword here is moderation. There are obvious health risks involved with heavy alcohol use and abuse, not the least of which is accidental death owing to drinking and driving. By moderation we mean one or two drinks daily—a cocktail before dinner or a glass of wine or beer with dinner.

Authorities have long wondered just why it is that those whom imbibe moderately enjoy a longer life. Today we believe it may be owing to alcohol's effect in increasing levels of the protective cholesterol, the HDLs. Those who have a drink or two daily tend to have significantly higher HDL levels, affording them an added margin of protection against heart disease.

All this is not to suggest that you start to drink if you don't already do so. Rather, if you now enjoy a drink or two, by all means continue to do so with the knowledge that not only will this practice do no harm, but it will also very likely provide some health benefits.

The same can't always be said for coffee. Studies comparing coffee drinkers with those who don't indulge show that heart-disease rates tend to be higher for caffeine lovers. This has been an area of some controversy, however, since the coffee drinkers often tend to be the same ones who smoke cigarettes and who may be under greater tensions and stress levels. Efforts to equate coffee drinking with cholesterol levels have been contradictory in their results, with no final conclusion reached. The fact remains, though, that caffeine is a drug everyone can and should do without. In a stressful world, the last thing one needs is 'coffee nerves'.

I keep a hot thermos of decaffeinated coffee near my typewriter at all times. I buy the kind made with the water process of decaffeination, since coffees decaffeinated through other processes can contain harmful chemicals, and use a bit more when I brew a cup in order to provide full, rich coffee flavour.

~ Finally our discussion of categories of foods brings us to salt. There's no question that most people eat too much. Between salt used in home food preparation and added at the table and that found in processed foods and fast foods, the average person consumes an excessive amount of salt and other forms of sodium.

The major health concern involving sodium is high blood pressure. That affects about 10 per cent of the population, whose blood pressure will rise or fall depending on the amount of salt in the diet. There's no question but that if your doctor has diagnosed hypertension you'd do well to greatly limit the amount of salt consumed.

For the rest of the population as well, cutting back on salt and sodium can have benefits. First, we don't know whether we are prone to develop high blood pressure later in life. Second, salt leads to fluid retention in the body and no one needs that extra burden.

After a while it may grow boring to hear the same nutritional advice over and over. Virtually every health authority has called for generalized reductions in the consumption of fat, saturated fat, cholesterol, salt, and sugar, along with moderation in alcohol use. But that universality of advice indicates that the recommendations have the weight of years of research and experience.

So many of our health ills can be at least partially linked to diet. Heart disease, high blood pressure, obesity, diabetes, some forms of cancer, and osteoporosis, are in part caused by and strongly affected by what we eat. All of us would benefit from some modification away from the average diet. And long before you realize the future benefits of a longer, healthier life, you'll simply start feeling better. With a good diet you'll experience more vitality, more energy, less tiredness, and far less digestive upset. After a while you'll wonder how you could have ever enjoyed eating the way you did, and, therefore, feeling the way you did. Good health and vitality are a joy in themselves, an absolute pleasure from day to day and year to year.

SPECIAL FOODS THAT LOWER CHOLESTEROL

As I stated earlier, what you do eat is as important as what you avoid, especially when it comes to lowering your cholesterol level to reduce your risk of heart disease. The first food shown to have potent cholesterol-lowering potential was oat bran, which is an essential component of the regime in my book *The 8-Week Cholesterol Cure*. In case you haven't read my book, here's some background on this marvellous food.

The wonders of oat bran

When *The 8-Week Cholesterol Cure* was first published, in 1987, one of the questions most asked by interviewers was 'What *is* oat bran?' No one asks that anymore. Oat bran has quickly become the food of choice for those concerned about cholesterol. For many months demand outstripped supply, and oat bran was actually hard to find. Happily, today oat bran is in ample supply.

The oat bran phenomenon began in the research laboratories of Dr James Anderson at the University of Kentucky in Lexington. At the time he was working with diabetic patients, trying to determine whether one cereal would be more effective than another in controlling blood-sugar levels. When Dr Anderson came to oatmeal, he found that not only were blood-sugar levels improved when participants ate oatmeal, but cholesterol counts fell as well.

Looking a bit more closely, Dr Anderson determined that it was the bran fraction of the whole oat flake that was responsible for this effect. Specifically, he found that the soluble fibre of oat bran does the job. It works by binding onto the bile acids, which are made of cholesterol and shunting them out of the body before they can be recycled. Thus the body must make more of those bile acids for the digestive process, and to do so it must turn to the cholesterol in the blood. Little by little, as more bile acids are eliminated and

more cholesterol is used to manufacture more bile acids, the
cholesterol level in the blood drops.

One of the special things about the way oat bran works is that
it lowers only the bad cholesterol, while levels of the good cholesterol, the HDLs, remain unchanged. This means an even better
ratio between total cholesterol and HDLs, ensuring increased
protection against heart disease.

How much effect can oat bran have in cutting into cholesterol?
In one study, men were fed 100 grams, a little more than 3 ounces,
daily. Their total cholesterol fell by 13 per cent. In a controlled
study in which six men ate all their meals under close supervision
in a metabolic ward, and consumed 100 grams of oat bran daily,
an amazing drop of more than 23 per cent was seen after just 21
days.

It appears that the cholesterol-lowering effects increase over
time. Administering an oat-bran diet in his laboratories, Dr
Anderson observed a 19 per cent drop. After the subjects returned
home, but continued to eat 50 grams of oat bran daily, cholesterol
levels fell by a total of 24 per cent.

Impressive results have been shown by researchers all over the
USA. Dr Dennis Davidson, then of the University of California
at Irvine and now at Stanford University, fed medical students
muffins daily. The students didn't know whether they were getting
oat-bran muffins or muffins made with wheat flour. The wheat
muffins produced no cholesterol lowering, while the oat-bran
muffins provided a significant reduction.

Since oat bran is part of the whole oat flake, one can expect
lowering of cholesterol levels with oatmeal as well. Remember that
was how Dr Anderson first determined this benefit. But, since the
'secret ingredient' is soluble fibre, and there is more soluble fibre
in the oat bran than in the oatmeal, one would need more
oatmeal—almost double the amount—to achieve the same effects
as with oat bran.

At Northwestern University in Chicago, Dr Linda Van Horn
studied the effects of oat bran and oatmeal as part of a low-fat diet,
and compared those results with low-fat diet alone. She found that
both oat bran and oatmeal provided an additional 3 per cent
reduction over the lowering achieved by diet alone. But that low
percentage of reduction was owing to the fact that the subjects in
the study had normal cholesterol levels to begin with. Individuals
with elevated cholesterol counts can expect a greater percentage
of improvement. And, at those higher cholesterol levels, it's

generally recognized that oat bran will provide more significant reduction than oatmeal.

While sceptical at first, the medical community has come to see the value of oat bran as part of a total cholesterol-reducing programme. Dr Bruce Kinosian at the University of Maryland's department of medicine compared the cost-effectiveness of treating patients with significantly elevated cholesterol levels with oat bran and the cholesterol-reducing prescription drugs colestipol and cholestyramine. He found that, in terms of lives saved by way of cholesterol reduction and thus lessened heart-disease mortality, oat bran was more cost-effective. He concluded in his report in the *Journal of the American Medical Association* in 1988 that cholesterol reduction by way of diet and oat bran 'may be preferred to a medically oriented campaign that focuses on drug therapy'.

Those consuming oat bran regularly report a very favourable side effect: weight control. There are a number of reasons why oat bran can help you to lose weight and to maintain ideal weight. For one thing, oat bran, either as cereal or muffins, satisfies the appetite more efficiently than other, higher-calorie foods. And, of course, those higher-calorie foods are replaced in the process. You'll find you just don't get as hungry when eating oat bran. A hearty bowlful in the morning for breakfast will satisfy you until lunch.

Hunger satisfaction depends largely on how quickly foods move through the digestive tract. As it happens, oat bran slows down the rate of the so-called 'gastric emptying', the time it takes to move out of the stomach. This adds to the feeling of fullness. Additionally, high-fibre foods provide more food mass in the small intestine.

Dr Anderson reports three reasons why oat bran may help in weight reduction. First, there is a certain amount of calorie loss directly through the faeces. Second, carbohydrates are not fully metabolized. And third, fibre-rich foods such as oat bran require more energy to digest, thus actually increasing the rate at which calories are burned. Compare that with fat calories, which authorities now feel provide more food energy than previously calculated, therefore requiring more activity to burn. While protein and carbohydrates yield 4 calories per gram, fat was long thought to supply 9. But that number may have been underestimated; it is now believed that the real figure may be closer to 10 or 11, possibly even 12 calories per gram.

On the down side, you might notice a bit of gassiness and

flatulence when you first start eating oat bran regularly, particularly if your diet has been low in fibre. For most people, that flatulence gradually diminishes. But, if it poses a particular problem for you, reduce the oat bran for a while and then gradually begin to increase the amount you eat daily.

You can find oat bran in the cereal section of practically every supermarket and health-food store. The package should list just one ingredient: oat bran. I advocate half a cup daily, measured uncooked as it comes out of the box. That weighs a little less than 2 ounces, about 50 grams.

Unfortunately there is no standard of identity for oat bran. The bran is the outer layer of the whole oat flake, just under the hull. First a manufacturer makes oatmeal by treating the whole grain with steam and then passing the grain between rolls to produce flakes. Grinding the oat flakes and sifting result in two milling fractions. There's a fine fraction, flour; and a coarse fraction, the oat bran. Some brands of oat bran contain only that coarse fraction, while others include varying amounts of the fine fraction along with it. This means that one brand will have more soluble fibre than another. In some instances, a company's oat bran will be no more than ground-up oatmeal. While that would still be a nutritious product, it won't deliver the cholesterol-lowering effect you're after. As so often is the case, you get what you pay for, and you may well be better off buying oat bran produced by a well-known company.

You'll also find a number of ready-to-eat oat-bran cereals on the market, some of which are better than others. Read the nutrition label carefully to see how much oat bran you're getting; is oat bran listed first, or third or fourth? Did the manufacturer add some fat that you don't want? Finally, check the actual fat content of the product. Oat bran itself has about 2 grams per 1-ounce serving. Does the product in question have more?

Is it best to eat your daily requirement of oat bran all at once, in the morning for example, or would you be better off with some oat bran throughout the day? Probably the latter, since bile acids are made throughout the day, and you'd do well to remove them throughout the day. With the recipes you'll find in this book, that's deliciously easy to do, with both oat bran and other foods rich in soluble fibres.

Oat bran's versatility makes it a natural in the kitchen. You may even want to put an oat bran canister next to your flour and sugar. It works beautifully in baking, can be substituted for bread crumbs in a number of recipes, and lends itself well to a variety of cooking situations.

I started experimenting with different ways to incorporate oat bran into my diet from the very start of my programme, since I've never been much of a cereal eater. So I played around with muffin recipes until I got them just right. A number of those recipes went into *The 8-Week Cholesterol Cure*. I didn't stop baking and cooking when the book came out, and over the years I've developed many more muffin varieties as well as other delicious baked goods. Then Michele Urvater contributed her expertise, and we now have found many new ways to cook and bake with oat bran. I hope you enjoy those recipes.

But oat bran is just one of the foods that provide a rich source of soluble fibre. Dried beans and peas, including chickpeas, pinto beans, kidney beans, black beans, red beans, white beans, black-eyed beans, split yellow and green peas, and on and on, provide soluble fibre as well.

Dried beans and peas

Dried beans and peas are a regular part of the daily menu in Middle Eastern countries, Africa, Latin America, and Europe and are becoming more popular in the U.K. When I spoke to Michele about developing some new recipes for these, she was delighted, for she loves to cook dried beans and peas and felt that people were really missing out by not knowing how to work with them. So I came up with a list of all the recipes I wanted. I'd enjoyed Cuban black beans, Cajun red beans, and many other ethnic specialities in restaurants but I didn't know how to cook them. I especially wanted recipes that were low in fat. And I didn't want recipes that called for hours and hours of cooking time. With that in mind, Michele went back to her kitchen and came up with several mouth-watering recipes.

We know that dried beans and peas work as well as oat bran in lowering cholesterol. Dr Anderson proved it in his University of Kentucky laboratories, where he fed subjects a daily diet rich in beans for three weeks. His volunteers ate a bit more than 100 grams of pinto and haricot beans daily as cooked beans or bean soup, and their cholesterol levels fell by an average of 19 per cent. Other studies have shown similar reductions, especially when beans are included in a low-fat diet.

At first blush, 100 grams seems like a lot of beans; after all, that's double the 50 grams of oat bran needed to supply the soluble fibre we want to lower cholesterol. But that 100 grams measures out to one-half cup of dried beans, the same as oat bran. The difference is that beans are heavier than oat bran.

Ultimately, we need to have the desired amount of soluble fibre provided by either oat bran or beans, or from other food sources as described in the coming pages. One day you may want three oat-bran muffins, and another day it'll be a bowl of oatmeal for breakfast and some beans as a side dish for dinner. Another day you'll have fruit for breakfast, with all your soluble fibre coming from an entrée featuring beans or peas. And we haven't even considered all those other food sources of soluble fibre yet. With so much potential variety, there's no reason to get tired of the foods that are not only good for you but that will actually drop your cholesterol level.

Barley

What could be more welcome on a cool evening in autumn than a steaming bowl of barley soup accompanied by some crusty bread and perhaps a glass of good white wine? Filled with vegetables, a bit of beef, and the barley, this soup is a meal unto itself. And barley also ranks as a cholesterol fighter.

Barley contains some soluble fibre, but as you'll see in the table on page 43, each 3½-ounce serving contains just 2.8 grams, which doesn't compare well with the 7.2 grams in the same amount of oat bran. Of course, every little bit helps. However, barley seems to have a capacity for cholesterol reduction far beyond what its soluble-fibre content would predict. Scientists are now at work trying to figure out just what it is about barley that makes it effective.

At the University of Wisconsin's Cereal Institute in Madison, Dr David Peterson reports isolating two compounds in barley's protein-rich outer portion that appear to have a potent cholesterol-lowering effect. Interestingly, that's the portion that is normally discarded in processing. The effect is different from that achieved by the soluble fibre. Those barley-derived substances work on the activity of the enzyme HMG Co-A reductase, which determines the amount of cholesterol made by the liver.

Working at the Miller Brewing Company in Milwaukee, Dr Frank Weber has found that barley-bran flour made from brewers' grain decreased total serum cholesterol by 44 per cent, but only when the lipid, or fat, portion of the barley grain was left intact. Defatted barley lacked cholesterol-lowering capability.

At this time, studies have focused entirely on laboratory animals. No human studies have been performed. Therefore no one can say exactly how much barley, as the whole grain or flour, would be needed to lower cholesterol levels. As time goes on, perhaps research will result in a drug or a food supplement derived from barley, or reveal the benefits of barley as part of the diet.

In the meantime, there's no reason not to include barley as part of a total programme of cholesterol reduction and good nutrition. You may not want to eat barley every day, but a look at the numerous recipes we've developed will show you some inventive ways to eat it more often than you likely do now. Today half of the barley harvested is used in brewing, and the other half goes to feed livestock; little barley finds its way into our diet. I think that will rapidly change, and you can be among the first to get on the bandwagon.

A is for apple

Leave it to American industry to come up with a way to improve on as basic a food as the apple. Now we all know that apples make a wonderful snack, that they're low in fat and high in fibre, and versatile in dozens of recipes. But did you know that the soluble fibre in apples, namely pectin, can lower cholesterol levels? Unfortunately, there's just a little bit of pectin in a medium-size apple, but now the apple industry has found a way to make this substance available in larger doses.

It all started when apple growers realized that, after squeezing apples to make juice and cider, they had to do something with the leftover pulp. In the past, that pulp was fed to livestock or disposed of as waste. In fact, it is a very concentrated source of both soluble and insoluble fibre. Then the Tastee Apple company of Newcomerstown, Ohio, came up with a way to dry the pulp and make it into a flourlike substance that can be used in a number of recipes. As you'll see, you can use it in baking muffins and biscuits and as an added ingredient in tomato sauce for a thicker, slightly sweet sauce.

Apple fibre contains nearly 43 per cent total dietary fibre. Of that amount, about 32 per cent is insoluble and 11 per cent is soluble. That means that you'll get a little more than 3 grams of soluble fibre per ounce. Compare that to a bit more than 1 gram of the soluble fibre, pectin, in a medium-size apple. It's also more soluble fibre than you get from oat bran! The bottom line is that apple fibre offers a wonderful alternative to oat bran.

But don't confuse apple fibre with pectin itself. You can find pectin, typically used for making jam, in supermarkets and health-food stores, but pure pectin does not lend itself to most recipes and simply won't work in the recipes we've developed for this book.

Do we have any proof that pectin can lower cholesterol levels as well as oat bran? Indeed we do.

Dr James Anderson of oat-bran research fame compared the effects of oat bran, guar gum, and pectin in terms of counteracting the blood-cholesterol increase expected when laboratory animals were fed dietary cholesterol. He found pectin to be the most efficient. None of the soluble fibres tested lowered the levels of protective HDL in the blood.

That study was done in 1979, before pectin was readily available in a form that could easily be worked into the diet. Using plain pectin was impractical in the dosages needed to get the desired effects. In a study that directly compared the effects of wheat bran, increased consumption of fruits and vegetables, and supplementation with citrus pectin, researchers found that citrus pectin reduced total serum-cholesterol levels significantly during the test period, while increased consumption of fruits and vegetables brought on a small but insignificant reduction.

Work in this area has been done all around the world. At the Institute of Human Nutrition in Czechoslovakia, Dr Emil Ginter gave a group of 21 healthy people with mildly elevated cholesterol levels a dose of 15 grams of citrus pectin for six weeks. He found a significant reduction in two-thirds of the patients.

We know that whether pectin is derived from citrus fruit or apples the effect is the same. Pectin is a soluble fibre that works exactly the same way as the soluble fibre in oat bran or dried beans and peas.

It shouldn't come as any surprise that the concentrated form of pectin provides more cholesterol-lowering capability than the smaller amounts found in apples. But that doesn't mean we can't derive additional benefits from eating fresh fruits and vegetables. As you'll see in the table on page 43, you do get some soluble fibre in a variety of foods. It all adds up. And you can't forget the nutrition provided in a balanced diet beyond the cholesterol-lowering effects of some foods. After all, man can't live by soluble fibre alone.

Today the availability of apple fibre, with the benefits of both soluble and insoluble fibre in a concentrated form, makes it possible and deliciously practical, to include apple pectin in the diet regularly. The same can now be said for another type of soluble fibre that has had much attention in the laboratory but until recently was impractical in real-life eating.

Apple fibre is a new food which may only be available in selected supermarkets and health food stores, but it is expected that this will be increasingly available in future as distribution networks are being set up by the American manufacturers.

Go for some guar gum

If you've been reading food labels, you may have noticed an ingredient called guar gum at the end of the listing for certain foods. And you may well have wondered what it is and what it's doing in food. The food industry uses guar gum as a natural thickening agent in foods such as yogurt, especially the nonfat variety, to give it extra body when the fat is removed.

Guar gum comes from the cluster bean, a plant in the legume family that grows well in arid regions such as Pakistan and certain areas of Texas. The plant bears pods containing six to nine beans that aren't very palatable. Guar gum is prepared by first removing the husk and the first layer of the beans, the endosperm, and then purifying the gum from the endosperm. The result is a powder that makes a gel in water.

The small amount found in various foods when used as a thickening agent has no effect on the body. But, when larger dosages are consumed, cholesterol levels fall. When the research first began, guar gum wasn't available to the general public. It was difficult to work with, since large amounts cooked into foods such as soups or stews became too thick to enjoy. Given as a powder to mix with water or juice, guar gum frequently caused gastric upset and nausea. Early studies used guar gum capsules to get the substance into the body, but even then it didn't disperse well in the digestive tract.

Even with those difficulties, guar gum was found effective in lowering cholesterol levels in study after study around the world. In one study, it was incorporated into a crispbread given to 11 patients over an eight-week period of time. About 12 grams of guar gum were actually consumed daily. Total cholesterol fell by

13 per cent while levels of LDL cholesterol came down by 16 per cent. Unfortunately, there were the gastric side effects I mentioned earlier.

In another study, guar gum was given in capsule form to 24 healthy volunteers. They took 9 grams daily for four weeks, while another group received placebo capsules. At the end of the month, those receiving guar gum experienced a 16.6 per cent drop in total cholesterol, and a 25.6 per cent fall in LDL cholesterol. Those getting the placebo capsules showed no change in cholesterol levels at all.

A study conducted in Italy showed that 16 grams daily given to 12 patients for two months resulted in an average cholesterol drop of 1.2 mmol, a 15 per cent decline. In Finland, a country with one of the highest heart-disease rates in the world, patients were given 5 grams of guar gum four times daily. After four weeks, cholesterol levels had fallen by 20 per cent. A Swedish study using 10 grams of guar gum twice daily demonstrated an average decline of from 6.2 to 5.7. And in Australia 17 patients completing a study with 6 grams three times a day showed a drop of 15 per cent. Two patients dropped out because of gastric upset.

More recently in America, a specially processed, palatable guar gum preparation was tested in 6 healthy subjects and in 17 diabetic patients. They received 10 grams twice a day. Total cholesterol levels fell by 14 per cent. But diabetic patients whose initial cholesterol counts were higher than 270 experienced a 26 per cent reduction. And levels of the protective HDL did not fall at all. Any gastic disturbances such as flatulence disappeared after about a week. In publishing that report, Dr Robert Superko of Stanford University wrote that guar gum provides a step between normal dietary intervention and the use of drugs to control cholesterol levels. Today we have guar gum formulations that are easily incorporated into the diet without gastric disturbances; in fact, guar gum can be used in a number of very enjoyable ways. It is available in capsules and powder, and plain and orange flavours allow you to consume it either as a beverage mixed with water or incorporated into a variety of shake recipes. Each teaspoonful of powder contains about 5 grams of soluble fibre. Based on the research to date, a total of 15 grams—one teaspoonful three times daily—would be expected to yield a considerable cholesterol benefit.

Rice bran

Rice has been grown for thousands of years, since well before the time of Christ and going back millennia in the Far East. Today rice remains the staple in the diets of more than half the world's population. Rice has a lot going for it: it's easily digestible, causes almost no allergic reactions, and is extremely versatile. But, as is recently becoming increasingly clear, there's even more to rice than we ever knew.

Mankind has long relied on rice as a major source of nutrients. Most people prefer polished white rice. Yet the bran layers of the rice kernel contain most of the nutrients, and that layer is discarded in processing rice to the polished white form. The highest nutrition, then, is available as brown rice, which has the bran fraction left in.

Until fairly recently, though, brown rice was the only way one could get the nutrition of rice bran, because when the bran was removed a biochemical reaction caused the bran to become rancid. So rice bran has traditionally been used exclusively as animal feed. However, a stabilization process originally developed by the US Department of Agriculture has led to the introduction of stabilized rice bran, which has a much-lengthened shelf-life. The product has a slightly sweet taste and crunchy texture. It can be used as is, sprinkled on top of other cereals and yogurt, baked into a variety of recipes, and pulverized to increase its versatility as you'll see in the recipes in this book.

But, beyond the general nutritive benefit of rice bran, it has the ability to lower cholesterol levels dramatically. For one thing, rice bran has a high concentration of soluble fibre. While it takes half a cup of oat bran daily to get enough soluble fibre to reduce cholesterol significantly, it takes only two tablespoons of rice bran to match that amount of soluble fibre.

Just as I was finishing the manuscript of this book, some exciting research data was being reported in New Orleans at the annual meeting of the Federation of American Societies for Experimental Biology. There Dr Robin Saunders of the US Department of Agriculture in Albany, California, told how rice bran was just as effective in reducing cholesterol levels as oat bran.

We can expect to hear more and more about rice bran in the future, as a number of studies are in progress or are in planning stages. But one of the most interesting aspects of Dr Saunders' work is that rice bran worked to cut cholesterol counts only when the oil fraction of the grain was left intact. When rice bran was defatted, it did not have a cholesterol-lowering effect at all.

Obviously, there's something about the oil in rice bran that does the job. And, as we saw just a bit earlier, the oil fraction in barley appears to have a cholesterol-cutting property. Oat bran, interestingly, has the highest fat content of any of the usual cereal grains. Look at the box and you'll see that each 1-ounce serving of oat bran has a full 2 grams of fat. But, since all that fat lowers cholesterol rather than raising it, we needn't even include those grams of fat into our daily fat-gram count.

But the rice story doesn't end there.

The Japanese have experimented with rice-bran oil for cooking, and have found that it has a dramatic effect on cholesterol levels as well. Dr Shinjiro Suzuki, of the National Institute of Nutrition in Japan, has fed various combinations of this oil to subjects over the years. His most recent findings indicate that a combination of 70 per cent rice-bran oil and 30 per cent safflower oil has the ability to drop cholesterol levels by 26 per cent when subjects consumed about half a cup daily. For reasons yet to be determined, that combination is more effective than either oil alone or any other combination, or, for that matter, any other edible oil in the world!

Half a cup of oil daily may seem like quite a lot, and for those attempting to limit the fat in the diet, it certainly is a large quantity. In Dr Suzuki's research, subjects consumed 60 grams daily. That's more fat than I eat from *all* food sources combined for the day. But many people simply will not cut their fat consumption that far. They like their fried foods, cookies, and salad dressings too much to do so. Now they have an alternative. Imagine French-fried potatoes prepared in rice-bran oil, which can lower your cholesterol count. And cookies using rice-bran oil instead of butter, which also reduces those numbers. It's certainly worth considering.

Rice-bran oil is bland-tasting, making it useful as a replacement for regular cooking oil. In fact, it has a very high smoke point, making it a natural for high-temperature cooking such as stir-frying in a wok.

Fish and fish oils

I remember having a talk with my father during the 1960s about the cholesterol controversy. Dad was a pharmacist and I had begun my career in medical writing, so both of us read about health issues regularly. The gist of the conversation was whether there was anything to this business of diet and heart disease. I recall very well bringing up the point that Eskimos ate a diet high

Fibre Content of Various Foods

Food	Total Dietary Fibre*	Soluble Fibre*
Grains		
Barley, pearl	10.8	2.8
Maize flour, whole-grain	15.3	9.0
Oat bran, uncooked	18.6	7.2
Oatmeal, uncooked	12.1	4.9
Rice, brown, dry	7.2	0.7
Rice bran	35.0	33.0
Fruits		
Apple, raw	2.0	0.6
Apple fibre	42.9	11.1
Prunes, dried	16.1	4.6
Raisins	6.8	1.7
Dried beans and peas		
Beans, kidney, canned	6.2	2.7
Beans, kidney, raw	19.9	8.5
Beans, pinto, raw	18.7	7.0
Beans, white, raw	16.2	4.7
Lentils, raw	16.9	3.8
Peas, black-eyed, raw	25.0	11.0
Peas, chick, raw	15.0	7.6
Peas, split, raw	11.9	4.0

*Grams per 100-gram serving (3½ ounces). Taken from *Plant Fiber in Foods* by James W. Anderson MD with permission from the Nutrition Research Foundation, Box 22124 Lexington, KY 40522, and others.

in fat and yet they had one of the world's lowest heart disease rates. Not very long after we had that chat, Dad learned that his cholesterol level was high, and the doctor advised a low-cholesterol diet, specifically recommending against the oysters Dad loved. We knew very little then, and Dad died in 1969 of a massive heart attack.

We've come a long way since those days. The Eskimos' high-fat diet actually protects against heart disease. And oysters definitely are back on the menu for even the most cholesterol-conscious person. Piece by piece, researchers have put together a mosaic of information that now shows us that just about all fish and shellfish have an important place in heart health.

It all began with research conducted in the 1970s by Danish

investigators, who wondered why the Eskimos could eat a diet rich in whale blubber, seal meat, and fatty fish and yet have virtually no heart disease. Danes with such a high-fat diet had a very high rate of that killer. And, when Eskimos left their homeland and migrated to Denmark, heart-disease rates soared. Obviously their genes didn't change in the boats during the trip away from home. The research conducted to find the answers to this enigma led to landmark reports casting a whole new light on how diet can protect against heart disease.

A closer inspection revealed that those marine fish and mammals are rich not in saturated fat but rather in the polyunsaturated forms. Specifically, the flesh of those creatures contains a class of fatty acids called the omega-3 fatty acids.

In working with the Eskimos, researchers noted that they had a tendency to bruise easily. It turns out the reason is that their blood platelets, those cells involved with clotting, are less sticky than is typical in Danes or Americans. Those scientists felt that the Eskimos were somehow protected from heart disease by whatever it was that was causing this difference in their blood. Interestingly, in studying blood samples further, they quickly saw that cholesterol levels were not much lower, if at all, than in Americans and Europeans who routinely succumb to heart attacks.

How does the platelet stickiness or lack of that stickiness make a difference? Platelets help to initiate the process of hardening of the arteries. First there is a bit of microscopic damage to the lining of the artery, frequently where blood flows turbulently around the bends and forks in the vessel. As part of the 'healing' process, platelets come to the site, stick to the injured surface, and release chemical signals that, in turn, cause muscle tissue of the artery to grow and attract white blood cells travelling in the blood. The growing mass of muscle cells and white blood cells then accumulates deposits of cholesterol, thus becoming bulky. We refer to that bulkiness of the arterial surface as plaque. As the plaque becomes larger and fills more of the interior of the artery, blood flow is reduced.

In an ideal scenario, the person perfectly protected against heart disease would have less cholesterol in the bloodstream to accumulate at those damage sites. And the person's platelets wouldn't be so sticky as to start the process in the first place.

We've learned, of course, that saturated fat in the diet is more responsible for the production of cholesterol than is dietary cholesterol itself. People consuming less saturated fat tend to have lower levels of cholesterol. That's one way of getting protection.

The Eskimos have another. Oil in the diet finds its way into the membranes of the body's cells. The fish oil they consume gets in the way of the cell's production of a certain kind of prostaglandin called thromboxane. The less thromboxane in the platelet, the less sticky it is, and the less clotting occurs. Moreover, fish oils stimulate the production of another prostaglandin, namely prostacyclin, which actually inhibits platelet clotting. This is the chemical scenario responsible for the Eskimos' abnormal bruising. The fish oil in the Eskimos' diet inhibits clotting in the same way that taking aspirin lessens clotting in many arthritis patients. In fact, arthritis sufferers often bruise quite easily. And, as an additional benefit, it appears that fish oil can act as an anti-inflammatory agent just as aspirin does.

You and I can't very easily find whale blubber and seal meat in our supermarket. But we can buy the fish richest in the oils now known to give heart-disease protection to the Eskimos. We'll look at the best choices for fish selection a bit later.

If the Eskimo research were the only evidence that fish should be on the menu of every heart-healthy man and women, there might be some doubt. Other factors may be playing a role in that particular population. But we now have proof from around the world.

Researchers from the University of Leiden in the Netherlands have been working with the population of the town of Zutphen since 1960 to examine the relations of diet and other risk factors to chronic diseases, including heart disease. Zutphen is an old industrial town in the eastern part of the country, with a population of 25,000 at the time the study began.

For the purposes of their study, investigators focused on 1088 men who had lived in the town for at least five years. They examined food intake in terms of quantity and types of food eaten. Risk factors, including serum cholesterol, smoking habits, blood pressure, physical fitness and activity, occupation, and height and weight were recorded. Just one of the many items listed as variables in the population was fish consumption.

The average Zutphen man consumed 20 grams of fish daily, about two-thirds of which was lean and one-third fatty. About 19 per cent of the men did not eat fish. Men with a high fish consumption had a significantly higher intake of monounsaturated and polyunsaturated fat, dietary cholesterol, animal protein, and alcohol in the diet than those who did not eat fish. Otherwise the fish eaters and abstainers were similar in their characteristics, both good and bad, pertaining to heart disease risk.

During 20 years of follow-up, 78 men died from coronary heart disease. Mortality from this disease was more than 50 per cent lower among those who consumed at least 30 grams of fish per day than among those who did not eat fish. Researchers studying the data found that the more fish the men ate, the more protection they had against heart disease and death. Conversely, the less fish consumed, the greater the risk.

It's particularly important to note that the protection apparently conveyed by fish was separate from any other considerations. In other words, after carefully looking at lifestyles, one could not come up with any other possibilities, such as that, perhaps, those who died were also heavy smokers. The fact remained after exhaustive statistical analysis of the data that fish was somehow involved in protecting those men who did not die by heart attack.

The conclusion reached by the researchers was that eating even a moderate amount of fish on a regular basis could be expected to convey that kind of protection. How much would be enough? Remember that the more fish eaten, the greater the protection demonstrated. But it would appear that two fish meals weekly would put one into the category termed fish eaters in this study.

Further evidence of fish's health benefits comes from Japan, whose population also enjoys a low rate of heart disease. Is that owing entirely to the low-fat diet, heavy in rice and vegetables? Research has shown otherwise. While it certainly remains true that low-fat diets pose less risk than high-fat diets, in Japan it has been demonstrated that those areas in which fish is regularly consumed have the lowest incidence of death by heart disease.

Most authorities today agree that the protection afforded by fish in the diet comes from the polyunsaturated omega-3 fatty acids, which are found almost exclusively in marine animals. One can find a small amount in certain plant sources but in the American diet, fish is the principal source.

Of the total omega-3 fats in fish, two types predominate: EPA, which stands for eicosapentanoic acid, and DHA, or docosahexaenoic acid. While authorities lean toward believing that the EPA is probably responsible for most of the effect enjoyed from fish oil, the DHA may well play an important role as well.

Moreover, there may be constituents of fish other than the omega-3s that are involved. The protection of the Eskimos comes from a diet almost exclusively derived from fatty fish and other animal sources, but the men of Zutphen eat lean fish, such as cod, most of the time. In other words, we just don't have all the answers yet. But we do know that a diet that includes two or three fish meals a week is good for the heart.

Taking a clue from the Eskimo, we'll want to select those types rich in oil, such as salmon, mackerel, anchovies, and sardines. Conversely, we needn't ignore such fish as cod and halibut just because they don't have a lot of oil. In fish, as in all foods, enjoy a wide variety.

That seafood variety can certainly also include shellfish. As explained earlier all shellfish, even shrimp, can be used as part of a low-cholesterol diet. Dr William Conner of the University of Oregon's Health Sciences Center has speculated that the potential detrimental effects of the cholesterol in shrimp may well be offset by the presence of the omega-3 fatty acids, even though there's just a tiny bit of fat in those delicacies. He sees no reason why shrimp can't be enjoyed in the same servings designated for chicken breast and fin fish. There are, however, a few seafood dishes one must be careful about. Caviar is high in both fat and cholesterol. For most of us, the price of caviar is enough to keep consumption down, and if I'm offered some Beluga caviar at a special cele-bration, I certainly don't turn it down! Squid contains about as much cholesterol in a 3½-ounce serving as you'd find in a large egg. That definitely makes it a once-in-a-while treat rather than a staple. The same applies to abalone, with more than 100 mg of cholesterol per 3½-ounce slice, especially if deep-fried or sautéed in butter. Yet, if you find yourself in northern California with fresh abalone on the menu, go for it. Just ask to have it sautéed in olive oil instead of butter.

The recipes included in this book should give you some new ideas for cooking fish. But what about taking a short cut to protection by way of fish-oil capsules? Virtually every medical authority agrees, and I concur, that the way to get fish oil into the diet is to eat more fish.

For one thing, those taking fish oil capsules still must make food choices. It makes little sense to continue eating foods rich in saturated fats and then swallow a few fish-oil capsules hoping to cancel out the effect of the fats. Actually, when taken in this way, fish-oil capsules can raise cholesterol levels rather than lower them. The fact remains that fish oil, whether from fish or from capsules, does not have a cholesterol-lowering effect at all. The protection afforded, as explained earlier, is by way of the clotting process. The oils do, however, lower triglyceride levels in the blood in individuals with elevations of those blood fats.

Fish supplies a wonderful nutrient profile; it is a great source of high-quality protein and vitamins. Fish-oil capsules provide no such nutrition.

Far too many questions remain concerning fish-oil capsules to recommend them blindly. How many capsules should one take daily? How much EPA should be in each capsule? Should the capsule also provide the DHA? If you're taking aspirin on the advice of your physician, do you also take fish oil capsules, knowing that they both inhibit clotting? Should women take fish-oil capsules if they're pregnant, breast-feeding or considering having a child, even though there is no data to show that the capsules are safe in such cases? The bottom line is that we have more questions than answers when it comes to fish-oil supplements.

The Eskimos eat fish, not capsules. So do the Japanese and the Dutch. Why not you?

I know a lot of people who say they really enjoy a wide variety of fish, but that they eat it only in restaurants. They don't know how to buy and properly cook seafood, and haven't the confidence to try. I hope the recipes in this book will get you started on a life of fish and seafood at home as well as away.

It all starts in the supermarket or wet fish shop. The place to buy seafood is the place that sells the most, so you can be sure of getting the freshest fish and seafood possible. Once you know and trust the person selling fish, ask what the freshest fish is for the day, and ask for tips on preparation. But until you develop that confidence in your fishmonger, here are some tips as to what to look for and what to avoid. To preserve freshness and moisture, fish should be displayed in cases filled with crushed ice. The fish should not be directly on the ice, nor near melting water. At home, keep fish and seafood on the top shelf of the refrigerator, where the temperature is coldest. Look for firm, elastic flesh with a nice, translucent colour and a moist, fresh-cut appearance. Fresh fish should not smell unpleasantly strong. Avoid soft, flabby fish, a milky colour, and any signs of drying.

The most important advice I can give about preparing fish is simply this: don't overcook. More than almost any other food, fish dries out quickly. I really believe that the reason some people say they don't like fish is that they have never had the opportunity to taste it properly prepared. All the reasons those people give for not liking fish—fishy flavour, dry, tasteless, poor texture—can be traced to poor fish selection and preparation.

People all over the world consume fish raw. While I'm not advocating that you eat raw fish, I'm pointing out that fish has a naturally delicate, flavourful nature. Just look at the popularity of sushi and sashimi. Most seafood cookbooks call for cooking fish about 10 minutes per inch of thickness, regardless of the method of preparation. I think that's too much cooking time. Also remember that the piece of fish will continue to cook internally until it is served.

When all is said and done, I personally think fish tastes best when grilled over charcoal. All those juices get sealed in and the taste is wonderful. And nothing could be simpler. Even the preparation of the coals is pleasant on a nice evening outdoors. During inclement weather, turn to the grill in the kitchen. In either case, count on no more than eight minutes per inch of total cooking time. Depending on the heat of the charcoal or your grill, you may even need less time.

Dry fish such as halibut will need a bit of oil brushed on each side. Salmon is as 'well-marbled' as a prime steak, and needs no additional oil.

Explore a variety of ways of preparing your fish. Each will give a slightly different texture to the fish, and I think each bestows a special flavour. If you've never tried poaching fish, give the method a try.

Of all the ways to prepare fish, I think this next one is the most unusual, and it's a terrific way to cook fish for a large group of people. Select a large salmon or other whole fish, counting on about 6 ounces per person. Get the freshest fish you can find. Wrap it in aluminum foil along with some thin-sliced lemon. Next put it into a large plastic storage bag, and close carefully. Then put it into your dishwasher! Set the timer, and that's all there is to it. At the end of the wash-dry cycle you'll have a beautifully prepared fish, done at exactly the right moment to serve your guests. Put it on a platter, set it on the table, and enjoy all the compliments you get. It's a no-fail approach.

What about leftovers? There are two ways to deal with leftover fish. First, if the steaks or fillets you've bought are too large for you, cut off the amount you don't want to eat for that meal. Wrap the extra fish in plastic wrap, putting it into a plastic storage bag, and then into the freezer. Accumulate a bit of fish here, an odd shrimp or scallop there, and you'll have a wonderful frozen assortment with which to make a fish soup such as bouillabaisse. Or use leftover cooked fish for tomorrow's lunch. Flake the fish and prepare sandwiches or salads in the same way you'd use chicken. There's no need for fish ever to go to waste.

While each fish and all the variety of shellfish have their distinct flavours and characteristics, all seafood lends itself to an array of seasoning possibilities, so keep your kitchen stocked with all the ingredients to prepare your seafood entrée for the day. Count on lemon, of course, but don't forget lime and orange for a change. Daubing fresh fillets with a good Dijon mustard prior to grilling yields a wonderful flavour. Flavourings that go particularly well with seafood include black peppercorns, fresh garlic, fresh or crystallized ginger, parsley, dill, and hot peppers. I think olive oil is best for sautéing. Use white wine for poaching. Fish prepared teriyaki style is a welcome alternative to chicken. Try unusual vinegars for something entirely different. Just remember that fish needs very little flavouring; its delicate flavour shouldn't be overwhelmed.

Let's look at some of the ways to cook fish and seafood in a bit more detail.

BARBECUING. This dry-heat method of cooking can be done on an open rack over charcoal, gas, artificial coals or what have you. Equipment can be anything from the most simple campfire to elaborate brick enclosures or imported barbecues. Barbecuing works well for fish because it cooks quickly and efficiently. Cooking outdoors can be a lot of fun. For something different, soak some hardwood chips in water and toss them on the coals to provide a deep smoky flavour.

BAKING/ROASTING. This is another dry-heat method of cooking; no liquid is added. It's best to bake or roast on a rack so that juices don't accumulate. Use a high heat, about 230°C/450°F/gas mark 8, so cooking is quick. Count on about 8 minutes per inch rather than the traditional 10 minutes.

GRILLING. While barbecuing refers to cooking over the heat source, grilling is done under the heat source. Salmon and other fatty fish may throw off quite a bit of smoke, and you should allow plenty of drainage for fat. For lean fish brush on a bit of oil.

POACHING. This is a virtually foolproof method of fish cookery in which seafood is cooked in simmering liquid just below the boiling point. You can poach in the oven or on the stovetop, with the dish covered or not. A variety of liquids—vinegar, wine, soya sauce—provide flavour and distinction.

STEAMING. Here we cook seafood over boiling water, not in it, so that the steam itself cooks the fish, which is held out of the water by a rack of some sort. Steamed fish needn't be plain: onions, lemon slices, and vegetables can be placed on top of the fish on the rack.

STIR-FRYING. With just a tiny bit of peanut or other oil, you can whisk small pieces of fish, shrimp, and other seafood in a wok to cook it wonderfully quickly. Prepare your vegetables in the same wok or frying pan and you'll have little clean-up time. Cook fish and other seafood just till the flesh loses its translucent colour and turns whitish.

OVEN-FRYING. If you love the crunchiness of fried food but hate the fat, this is the method for you. Coat pieces of seafood with oat bran, or crumbs, and brush with vegetable oil. Place on a baking sheet in a hot oven 230°C/450°F/gas mark 8 till the crust is crunchy. Serve with some seafood sauce.

MARINATING. Using vinegar, citrus juice, or other acidic liquid, you can 'cook' seafood without the use of heat. The acid denatures the protein, much the same way heat would. While the risk remains quite small, this method of seafood preparation does not kill all micro-organisms. Marinating before cooking gives fish a fine flavour.

MICROWAVING. Fish will cook at high power in just 3 to 5 minutes, depending on the size and power of your microwave oven. As you cook more fish, the time for cooking increases.

STEWING. Even if you've never cooked fish in your life but you've made stews and soups, you can succeed on your first try in preparing seafood soups and stews. Just remember that all seafood is delicate and requires very little cooking. First cook the vegetables and other ingredients, then add fish and shellfish during the last few minutes. This is simple yet elegant cookery.

When you multiply all the different kinds of fish and seafood by the number of cooking and seasoning methods at your disposal, it's easy to see that you never have to get tired of this wonderful food. Delicious, nutritious, and heart-protecting, there's nothing to match fish and seafood.

THE SHOPPING LIST

A few years ago, after learning that my son Ross's cholesterol level was elevated at the age of seven, I told him that eating a heart-healthy diet was going to get easier and easier. More and more people, I explained, were changing their eating habits, and the demand for low-fat, low-cholesterol foods would grow steadily. The food industry, spotting an economic niche to be filled, would satisfy that demand. Happily, we're seeing that happen as new and improved foods fill the supermarket shelves. Today we have low-fat, low-cholesterol options we never had before.

The dairy list
How low do you want to go? Today you have the choice to go all the way from whole-milk dairy products down to the completely fat-free foods. Lest you shock your tastebuds and get discouraged, gradually wean yourself from the high-fat milk. If you use whole milk now, go to 2 per cent fat, down to 1 per cent fat, and finally graduate to skimmed milk. As the old saying goes, yard by yard it's very hard, but inch by inch it's a cinch.

For other dairy foods, a gradual change isn't necessary. You can start making the switch during your next trip to the supermarket. Look for 1 per cent fat cottage cheese, with just 1 gram of fat per serving. There's no reason to eat more fat than that, since this product delivers all the flavour you want, with amazing creaminess.

Sour cream is almost by definition a high-fat food. But you can cut out a lot of that fat by reading the labels of some of the reduced-fat sour creams many local dairies now produce. You can cut the fat grams per serving by mixing equal portions of the sour cream with low-fat plain yogurt. With chopped chives, the mixture tastes terrific on a steaming baked potato.

You'll also find a number of brands of delicious very low-fat yogurt in a wide variety of flavours. Don't be put off by the formidable ingredients listed on some labels; guar gum, carra-geenan, and zanthan gum are natural, vegetable-derived thickeners.

For dessert, as suggested earlier, opt for frozen yogurt rather than ice-cream, since even the lowest-fat ice-creams can't com-pare once you know what that saturated fat does to your arteries. Even my children love going out to get some frozen yogurt, and they don't miss ice-cream at all.

Cheese contributes much of the saturated fat and cholesterol to the Western diet, so choose the low-fat types.

Last, and I do mean last, on the dairy food list is butter, which is nothing more than a concentrated mass of saturated fat and cholesterol. This is a passé product that doesn't belong in any heart-healthy person's diet. Here you have two alternatives.

Margarine is butter's logical successor. Today's margarines have wonderful flavour and texture. Just a few are made with unhealthful ingredients as tropical oils or animal fats. Read the labels. And as for those using 'partially hydrogenated' soybean or corn oil, today we know that the hydrogenation processes used by manufacturers to harden oils into tub margarine actually are not harmful. However, since total fat is also a consideration, look for fat-reduced margarines.

The meat list
The first thing many people think of when modifying the diet to cut back on fats and cholesterol is red meat. While it's true that beef has been a major source of saturated fat, there's no need to eliminate this nutritious food entirely. Many of your favourite recipes probably call for minced beef. If this is labelled as lean, it will usually still contain 10 to 15 per cent fat. But you don't have to settle for that. Instead, choose a very lean cut of beef and ask your butcher to trim off all the visible fat, even if that means cutting into the meat a bit. Then ask him to mince it. I like to get several pounds at one time, which I can ask the butcher to wrap in individual one-pound packages for the freezer, and I can prepare patties for hamburgers and meatballs for future use. This minced beef can be as low as 5 per cent fat.

The only way you can do better than that would be to have your butcher mince a skinned and boned turkey breast. Some butchers may balk at mincing turkey, since the equipment must be cleaned between different kinds of meat. I get around this by purchasing a large quantity at one time, again storing the minced turkey breast in one-pound packages in my freezer for future use. While he's at it, I ask the butcher to cut some of the turkey breast as cutlets, which I use in a number of recipes that would call for veal. Although veal is lower in fat than beef, turkey is even leaner.

But what about steaks and roasts? There are times when only a nice cut of red meat will fill the bill. I'm thinking especially about those evenings when I want to barbecue a steak over the charcoal in my backyard. For a long while after I began my quest for heart health and a low cholesterol level, I limited my steak splurges to just a few times a year. I did use some beef in certain recipes in limited quantities, but a piece of meat sizzling over the coals was a rare treat.

Today I enjoy those steaks and roasts on a regular basis, thanks to a welcome development in the American beef industry. Producers in various parts of the country have concentrated on delivering ultra-low-fat beef, raised without hormones, pesticides, or antibiotics. Steaks are as low in fat as fish or chicken breast. The problem in the past was that if a steak was low in fat it was also low in flavour, juiciness, and tenderness. Employing special techniques, today's producers of low-fat beef deliver all the flavour and tenderness you crave. One caution, however. This new beef dries out fairly easily, and doesn't work very well for those who want their steaks well done.

Pork offers fewer options, since most of it comes with a hefty dollop of fat. But the remarkable exception is ham. You can enjoy dinners of ham steaks, sandwiches of thin-sliced ham, and breakfasts of ham or lean bacon, all of which is extremely low in fat. Just look at the labels of ham products in your supermarket and select those with very low fat contents.

Our ancient ancestors, the cavemen, ate lots of meat, but the meat that they ate was different from that sold in today's supermarkets. It was much lower in fat, and probably lower in cholesterol as well, since it came from animals in the wild, which are leaner than our domesticated livestock. Can we enjoy the same kind of meat? Actually we can, whether or not we know any hunters. All wild game is low in fat and whether the hunter's prize is deer, rabbit, or game birds, you can eat it to your heart's content. Even domestic rabbit packs little fat, with baked rabbit yielding only 5 grams of fat per 3½-ounce serving.

Of course, in addition to beef and poultry, you'll want to include a variety of seafood in your monthly menu.

Although eggs provide the same high-quality protein as meat, they also supply a huge portion of cholesterol per yolk. Some egg producers are now saying that early cholesterol measurements weren't accurate, and that a large egg contains 'only' 200 milligrams of cholesterol instead of the previously listed 274 milligrams. But the reality remains that no one trying to control his or her cholesterol level should consume more than 300 milligrams of cholesterol daily. That means that even at the lower level one egg yolk just about shoots the cholesterol allowance for the day, leaving you with non-animal sources of food for the balance of that day.

Your option for eggs is the use of only the egg whites. Egg whites contain no cholesterol at all, and two egg whites in place of an egg works well in most dishes.

When baking muffins or other goods, here's a trick for making them come out lighter and fluffier. Don't just add the white to the rest of the moist ingredients and stir into the recipe. Instead, beat the egg whites till fluffy, and fold them into the recipe batter. It takes a bit more effort but the results make the work worth it.

Last but certainly not least in selecting protein foods, don't forget the lowly dried beans and peas. As discussed earlier, these are excellent sources of soluble fibre as well. With the tremendous variety of dried beans and peas, one could realistically include them in practically every day's menu. One day it might be soup, another day stew, the next day salad, and some days an entrée featuring beans. I think you'll enjoy the recipes that follow.

The bread and cereal list

At first glance, you wouldn't think that this food group would cause much trouble in the fat and cholesterol departments. Unfortunately, foods in this category are frequently a source of hidden fats. The only way to know which are healthful and which are hurtful is to read the labels carefully.

One package of rolls will be made with soybean oil while another lists animal shortening. Certain brands of cereal—even those made with oat bran—contain significant amounts of coconut oil. Bakery-shop goods typically bear no ingredient or nutrition labels, but are most often made with butter.

Happily, however, with a little scrutiny you can find breads and cereals that are truly heart-healthy. Many manufacturers have responded to consumer concerns by removing the offending fats and oils from their products.

Certainly oat bran will be high on your list of foods in this category. But read the labels to make sure you're getting the genuine article, not a product that contains a number of other ingredients. For the recipes in this book you'll need pure oat bran and oatmeal. That doesn't mean, though, that you need to avoid completely cereals that contain a number of ingredients. Those will add variety and nutrition to the diet, but they won't supply all the oat bran you need for the day.

Similarly, you'll want to stock your kitchen with whole-grain cereals and flours from grains other than oats as well. Wheat, for example, contains little soluble fibre, but is an excellent source of insoluble fibre, and we do need both.

In general, pasta offers a terrific way to get complex carbohydrates with little fat and no cholesterol. The many types provide tremendous variety.

The fruit and vegetable list

We have practically no limitations in this category of foods. Nutritionists have calculated that adults need two servings of fruit and two of vegetables daily as a minimum. The word to stress there is *minimum*. Depending on your calorie needs, you can have as many servings as you like.

Go for the variety and find shops with the widest choice. Whenever possible, fresh is best. You'll get all the nutrients and all the flavour the vegetables and fruits have to offer. Next best are frozen fruits and vegetables, and as a last choice, canned. Just be a bit cautious and avoid fruits canned in heavy syrup rather than in natural juices and water, and vegetables canned with a lot of sodium.

No fruits or vegetables contain any cholesterol at all, and only olives and avocados supply a large percentage of their calories as fat. Because I'm such a fan of guacamole, and I limit the amount of avocado I eat, we've included here a recipe for a type of 'guacamole' that has no avocados.

Practically every restaurant offers a fruit platter on the menu, and when it arrives at the table the appearance is enough to set anyone's mouth watering. But you needn't wait till you're dining out. Slice two or three types of fruit, arrange the pieces attractively, garnish with a bit of lettuce, and place a little dish of yogurt or cottage cheese in the centre.

The dessert list

I must admit that I miss desserts in restaurants. While I love fresh fruits and berries, I still hanker after all the gooey, elaborate concoctions. Maybe one day restaurants will offer more healthful versions of those desserts. But in the meantime you can enjoy sweet treats at home.

We've included some wonderful dessert recipes in this book, and remember, too, that dessert recipes in magazines and other cookbooks can be easily modified. You can replace half the flour in cake recipes with oat bran; this works particularly well in heavy cakes, such as carrot and banana cakes. Use egg whites in place of whole eggs. Use margarine or oil instead of butter; frequently you can get by with quite a bit less shortening than called for.

Very low-fat frozen yogurt makes an excellent replacement for ice-cream. Try topping it with fresh berries, and perhaps just a touch of liqueur. Chocolate yogurt topped with raspberries and a splash of Chambord (raspberry liqueur) is simply elegant, as is vanilla yogurt with a drizzle of crème de menthe.

Be far more careful with snack bars touted as being healthful. Frequently they include such ingredients as tropical oils, which you certainly don't want in your diet at all. Don't let advertising phrases like 'all natural' and 'organic' fool you. Read the labels carefully.

Kitchen equipment

One of the best investments you can make as you plan a healthful diet is sensible, useful kitchen equipment. You'll probably notice that as you buy fewer and fewer processed and prepared foods, you'll see savings in your food budget. Why not invest those savings in a piece of equipment that will make it easier for you to enjoy a wide variety of good food? Little by little your collection will grow, and with it your enjoyment of a low-fat diet.

For openers, you'll save a lot of fat by using non-stick Teflon pans or those with other coatings. You'll be able to use two or three of them in different sizes for sautéing and frying foods.

Sharp knives make short work of slicing and chopping vegetables and fruits. A good set of knives lasts a lifetime. And a good sharpener, either manual or electric, keeps the edges ready for action at the cutting board.

When first introduced, food processors were expensive and considered a luxury. Today the prices have come down and you'll find a hundred uses for the equipment. Vegetables for Chinese stir-fry, for example, can be prepared in just a few minutes.

If you don't already use a steamer for seafood and vegetables, just purchase a little folding steamer rack that can go inside a large covered pot. There's no need to use an expensive one. You'll find such racks in the housewares section of almost every supermarket.

While dry pasta remains an old standby, fresh pasta provides a special taste treat. The problem is that fresh pastas are usually made with whole eggs, bringing a lot of cholesterol to otherwise healthy food. The answer is to make your own fresh pasta with a pasta maker, and if you really enjoy pasta you'll find the varieties of pasta you can make to be truly delicious. If you have children, they'll love helping.

We eat food because it tastes good. Sure, we know that food contains the nutrients we need for health, growth, and maintenance. But the reason we eat it, without any special prompting, is because it pleases the palate. Those foods we find distasteful we conveniently omit from our diets. Very few people eat certain foods just because they're 'good for you'.

Today we know that a wide variety of food is good for us. And some of that food, as we've seen, can actually lower our cholesterol levels. But to eat it on a regular basis it has to taste good.

That's where the next section of this book comes in. The recipes we've included here are designed to make healthful food as palate-pleasing as possible. Whether for breakfast, lunch, dinner, or snacks, the dishes you'll prepare will give you a delicious new perspective on cholesterol control. Enjoy!

PART TWO

NOTE: *Special cholesterol-lowering ingredients are indicated throughout the recipes by lightface type.*

RECIPES LISTED BY SPECIAL INGREDIENTS

Dried Beans and Peas

Rice Bran

Apple Fibre

Oatmeal

APPETIZERS AND HORS D'OEUVRES

Three-Colour Bean Pâté

Makes 1 loaf, about 12 slices

In the old days, before I saw the light about changing my diet, I loved pâtés of all sorts, and indulged to my heart's content. Then I began to avoid the obvious offenders such as those made with liver, sticking with vegetable pâtés—until I learned that they are almost always made with eggs. Now I enjoy pâté made at home. It's fresher and, to be honest, a lot tastier.

275g/10oz cooked green split peas
2 teaspoons dried mint
3 tablespoons skimmed milk
3 sachets gelatine
275g/10oz freshly cooked or tinned chickpeas *or white cannellini beans, **drained***

3 tablespoons reduced-calorie mayonnaise
1 tablespoon lemon juice
275g/10oz freshly cooked or tinned kidney beans, drained
3 tablespoons chilli sauce

Lightly grease a 20×10cm/8×4in loaf tin.

Place peas, with mint and skimmed milk in a blender or food processor and blend until smooth.

Place one sachet of gelatine in a small saucepan and pour over 2 tablespoons cold water. Over low heat, dissolve geleatine in water until mixture is translucent and warm. Remove from heat, add to peas, and process until smooth. Spoon mixture into bottom of loaf tin and place in fridge for 10 minutes to set lightly.

Meanwhile, purée chickpeas or white beans with mayonnaise and lemon juice. As before, dissolve a sachet of gelatine in 2 table-spoons of water in a small saucepan. Heat gently until gelatine is translucent and warm and add to chickpeas or beans; process until smooth. Spoon this mixture on top of the green-pea mixture in loaf tin. Return loaf tin to the fridge to let the second layer set for 10 minutes.

Gently warm last sachet of gelatine in 2 tablespoons of water over low heat until translucent and warm. Purée kidney beans with chilli sauce and gelatine until smooth. Spoon this mixture over white layer of beans, and level the top. Cover and chill overnight.

Gently unmould the pâté and cut into slices.

Hummus (Chickpea Bean Dip)

This is the only recipe repeated from *The 8-Week Cholesterol Cure*. Just in case you don't have that book, I want you to have this wonderful Middle Eastern bean dip. Serve it to company or keep it in the fridge for quick snacks with wedges of toasted pitta bread. I haven't tired of this in nearly five years, and you can almost always find a supply in my fridge.

4 tablespoons tahini paste   *3 tablespoons water*
3 tablespoons lemon juice   *½ teapoons ground cummin*
5 cloves garlic, finely chopped   *2 × 430g/15oz tins chickpeas,*
5 drops Tabasco   *drained*

Simply combine all ingredients and blend until smooth. A food processor makes this really easy; use the large metal blade. Otherwise use a large bowl and electric mixer.

Green Hummus

Makes about 450g/1lb

Maybe one of the reasons there's so little heart disease among people of the Middle East is that they eat plenty of hummus. This variation is great for parties because of its wonderful emerald colour. If you plan to serve it to guests, assemble it at the last moment, or at least hold off on the lemon juice until you're ready to serve, because the lemon's acid will dull the bright green of the spinach to a drab olive colour. Serve as a dip with wedges of toasted pitta.

*225g/8oz fresh spinach or 2
  bunches watercress, de-
  stalked
2 tablespoons coriander or
  parsley leaves
275g/10oz cooked or tinned
  chickpeas, drained*

*2 tablespoons tahini
1 large clove garlic
3 tablespoons lemon juice
Cayenne pepper or Tabasco*

Whiz all the ingredients together in a food processor or blender until smooth. Place in fridge until ready to serve.

Bean and Mushroom Dip

Makes about 450g/1lb

275g/10oz cooked or tinned
   pinto beans, drained
100g/4oz raw mushrooms,
   finely chopped
2 stalks celery, finely chopped

1 teaspoon cumin powder
100g/4oz green chillies,
   chopped
¼ teaspoon garlic powder
Pepper to taste

Mix all the ingredients together in a food processor or an electric mixer. Cover and chill until ready to use.

Herb and Yogurt Dip

Makes about 450g/1lb

Here's a dip that combines the soluble fibre of oat bran with chickpeas. You might try toasting the oat bran first for added flavour, but the recipe will work well if you omit this step. Serve with toasted pitta triangles or tortillas, or as a sandwich spread.

25g/1oz oat bran
250ml/8fl oz low fat yogurt
2 spring onions
½ green pepper
2 tablespoons fresh dill, basil,
*　or coriander leaves*

3 tablespoons fresh parsley
1-2 teaspoons each dried
*　tarragon and mint*
225g/8oz cooked chickpeas
2 teaspoons Worcester sauce
Pepper

Heat a heavy frying pan, over medium-high heat, without any fat in it. After about 3 minutes, add oat bran. With a wooden spoon, stir continuously for 3 to 4 minutes or until the oat bran has a lovely toasted, nutty aroma.

In a food processor or blender, mix until smooth all the ingredients, including the toasted oat bran.

Spicy Roasted Chickpeas

Makes 450g/1lb

To make this recipe turn out as tasty and terrific as possible, use soaked and cooked dried chickpeas; the canned ones are too soft. You can serve them as appetizers, as an accompaniment, or just as something to munch on for an evening snack.

225g/8oz dried chickpeas,
*　soaked by quick or slow*
*　method (see Master Recipe*
*　for Boiled Dry Beans)*

2 egg whites
Barbecue seasoning, to taste

Slowly cook soaked chickpeas for 45 minutes or until just tender but with still some bite to them. Drain through a sieve and cool for 10 minutes.

Preheat oven to 160°C/325°F/gas mark 3.

Blend egg whites with barbecue seasoning and mix this into the chickpeas, coating them as evenly as possible. Pour chickpeas into a baking tin lightly greased with oil, and bake for 1 hour, stirring occasionally.

Remove from the oven, cool to room temperature and serve. They may be stored, in a covered jar, in the fridge. Bring to room temperature before serving.

MASTER RECIPE FOR BOILED DRY BEANS

Use this as the master recipe for cooking dried beans.
Although it takes some time to cook beans from scratch, they
have much more flavour and better texture when cooked this
way. They can be cooked in large batches, then frozen, for
up to 5 months. A pressure cooker is an invaluable aid for
cooking beans; most beans will be done in 15 minutes.

Step 1. Soaking

When using dried beans (not lentils or split peas), soak them
first to soften them, to cut down on the cooking time, and to
make them more easily digestible. There are two soaking
methods:

LONG SOAK: Cover the beans by three times their volume
in water and let them soak, overnight. Drain the beans and
use fresh water to cook them. Much of the flatulence
ascribed to beans is due to the soaking water, not the beans.
QUICK SOAK: Cover the beans by three times their volume
in water and bring the water to a boil; boil for 1 minute. Turn
the heat off and soak them for 1 hour only. Drain them and
use fresh water to cook them.

Step 2. Cooking the beans

Place the soaked beans in a saucepan with just enough water
to cover and bring the water to a simmer. Do not add acidic
ingredients, such as lemon juice, vinegar, wine, or tomatoes,
until the beans are already tender or the cooking time will
be lengthened and the beans will remain tough.

Keep the beans covered with liquid as they cook but do not
add any more than necessary or they can become water-
logged and their flavour will diminish.

225g/8oz of dried beans yields about double the quantity,
except for limas, which will yield rather more.

Time it takes to cook various types of beans, after soaking time

ADUKI: Small red oval beans from Japan; take 1 to 1½ hours to cook.

BLACK BEANS: Can be used instead of red kidney beans in various dishes. take 1½ hours to cook.

BLACK-EYED BEANS: Need no soaking; take 1 to 1½ hours to cook.

CHICKPEAS: Nutty-flavoured; take 1½ to 2 hours to cook.

BROAD BEANS: Take 1½ to 2 hours to cook.

WHITE BEANS, CANNELLINI: Kidney-shaped; take 1 to 1½ hours to cook.

KIDNEY BEANS, large and small: take 1½ hours to cook.

BUTTER BEANS: Flat and kidney-shaped; take 45 minutes to 1 hour to cook.

MUNG BEANS: Round and small, olive-coloured; take 30 to 45 minutes; often used for sprouting.

HARICOT BEANS: Hold shape well after long cooking; used in baked dishes; take 1½ hours to cook.

PINTO BEANS: Savoury taste; mild; take 1 to 1½ hours to cook.

Fat-Free Guacamole

Maybe it's because I live in California that I dearly love guacamole. Unfortunately, this delicious dip comes loaded with fat from the mashed avocados. When I see some at parties, I can't resist having a little, but I'd like to really dig in! The answer was to develop a recipe that was not only free of fat but also a good source of soluble fibre. This is it! Enjoy it with tortillas. Bake the tortillas for 8 to 10 minutes or until crisp.

*275g/10oz cooked green split
  peas, drained and chilled*
*1 tablespoon chopped spring
  onion*
2 tablespoons lime juice
1 large clove garlic, crushed

*1 small tomato with seeds
  removed*
100g/4oz green chillies
Tabasco to taste
Green food colouring, optional

Preparation couldn't be more simple. Just place all the ingredients except for Tabasco and green food colouring in a food processor or blender and blend until smooth and creamy. If the colour isn't quite green enough, add one drop of food colouring at a time and blend until nice and green. Then add Tabasco to taste.

Cabbage Strudel

Makes 1 strudel: 10 to 12 hors d'oeuvre portions

If you've been looking for something really different, this is it. Serve this as part of an hors d'oeuvre. This dish takes a bit of time, but it's well worth the effort.

450g/1lb Dutch or Savoy
  cabbage, cut into thin slices
  as for cole-slaw
1 onion, thinly sliced
250ml/8fl oz white wine
2 teaspoons caraway seeds
200g/7oz cooked or tinned
  *haricot beans, **drained***

Pepper
1 tablespoon olive oil
10 frozen filo leaves, defrosted
450ml/¾ pint tomato sauce,
  optional

In a large saucepan, simmer cabbage, onion, white wine, and caraway seeds, covered, for 45 minutes to an hour or until tender. Stir in beans and season to taste with pepper.

Preheat oven to 190°C/375°F/gas mark 5.

Pour oil into a small dish and get a pastry brush ready.

Lay 2 filo leaves, slightly overlapping, on a work surface and very lightly brush with oil. Lay another 2 leaves on top of the first and brush again with oil; repeat until all 10 leaves have been used.

Form cabbage-and-bean mixture into a sausage shape down the centre of the filo, leaving a border of 5cm/2in at each end. Fold one side flap of leaves over the cabbage and beans, then fold the end flaps over, and roll up the strudel. Place it, seam side down, on a baking sheet. With a sharp knife, make 4 or 5 slashes on top, to let the steam escape. Brush top of strudel with remaining oil and bake for 45 minutes.

Cool for 10 minutes, to let it set before slicing into it.

Sardine Dip

You won't believe this recipe is actually good for you! It's simple to prepare, yet elegant. Try eating it on fresh bagels, as a dip for raw vegetables, or as a sandwich spread.

120g/4oz tin smoked sardines
120g/4oz tin sardines, packed
  in water, drained

3 tablespoons low fat yogurt
1 spring onion, thinly sliced
1 tablespoon lemon juice

Drain canned sardines and pat them well with paper towels to absorb excess oil. Blend smoked sardines with other sardines, yogurt, onion, and lemon juice, in a food processor or an electric mixer. Mix until smooth and chill for 1 hour before serving.

Salmon Mould with Dill

Makes about 8 servings

Here's a healthy version of a classic recipe for entertaining, but once you try it you won't want to wait to have company over to make it again. You can use a ring mould or a fancy fish-shaped mould for a festive touch. Serve on leaves of lettuce, with cherry tomatoes and parsley as garnish. Leftover salmon mould makes a terrific sandwich spread.

1 teaspoon corn oil
1 sachet gelatine
175g/6oz tinned salmon,
  packed in water, drained
Juice of 1 lemon
1 spring onion
2 tablespoons fresh dill finely
  chopped or 1 teaspoon dill
  weed

1 teaspoon Worcestershire
  sauce
3 tablespoons low fat yogurt
50g/2oz oat bran or rice bran
For garnish: tomato wedges,
  watercress, fresh dill
  (optional)

Brush the oil over a 900ml/1½ pint mould.
  Sprinkle geleatine over 350ml/12fl oz water in a saucepan and leave for 1 minute.

In a food processor or blender, purée salmon, lemon juice, onion, dill, Worcestershire sauce, and bran until smooth. Blend in yogurt gently by hand.

Gently heat gelatine and water until the liquid is clear and feels hot to the touch; do not let it boil. Add gelatine and water to the salmon mixture and whirl together until smooth; pour into the prepared mould.

Cover and chill for 2 hours or until set. To unmould, dip bottom of mould in a bowl filled with hot water for a few moments; turn mould upside down onto platter. You can decorate or serve with tomato wedges, watercress sprigs, and fresh dill.

Potted Mackerel

This recipe provides a delicious way to get healthy fish oils into the diet. It can also be made with tinned salmon. Serve with crackers or use it as a sandwich spread.

400g/14oz smoked mackerel,
skinned and boned
3 tablespoons low fat yogurt
2 tablespoons ketchup
1 tablespoon sliced jalapeno
pepper

2 tablespoons chopped red
pepper
1 teaspoon chilli powder

In a food processor blend all the ingredients together until smooth. Place in small ramekins and chill for 2 hours. Serve as an hors d'oeuvre.

SOUPS

Curried Bean and Brussels Sprout Soup

'One Cup' Haricot Bean and Ham Soup

Bean Vichyssoise

Black Bean Soup

Black Bean and Onion Soup

Garbure

Swedish Yellow Split Pea Soup

Split Pea, Carrot, and Chicken Soup

Split Pea and Potato Soup

Three-Bean Soup with Celery and Lemon

White Bean Minestrone

Hearty Chickpea Soup with Ham

Portuguese Chickpea and Kale Soup

Chicken and Bean Gumbo

Southern Haricot Bean and Sweet Potato Soup

Pasta e Fagioli

Provençal Bean and Garlic Soup

Indian Lentil Mulligatawny Soup

Lentil, Potato, and Ham Soup

Turkey, Barley, and Lentil Soup

Barley, Ham, and Carrot Soup

Scotch Broth

Mushroom, Barley, and Haricot Bean Soup

Russian Beetroot and Barley Bortsch

Scottish Cock-a-Leekie Soup

Greek-Style Chicken Lemon Soup

Sweetcorn and Chilli Soup

Cream of Cauliflower Soup

Cream of Spinach Soup

Cream of Cabbage and Apple Soup

Chilled Tomato and Vegetable Soup

Salmon Chowder

Curried Haricot Bean and Brussels Sprout Soup

Makes 6 servings

Want a different way to have your vegetables tonight? How about drinking them as soup? The mixture of the beans with the Brussels sprouts is a delight, and the curry adds a real zing.

150g/5oz haricot beans **soaked**
  (see page 80)
1 tablespoon **curry powder**
1 teaspoon **garlic powder**
250ml/8fl oz **no salt added tomato sauce**
400g/14oz **Brussels sprouts, trimmed, and roughly chopped**

Pepper
2 tablespoons **finely chopped fresh parsley**
250ml/8fl oz **low fat yogurt**

In a medium saucepan, bring soaked beans, curry powder, garlic and 1.25 litres/2¼ pints water to the boil. Reduce to a simmer and cook gently, partially covered, for 1¼ hours.

Add tomato sauce and Brussels sprouts, and simmer for 15 minutes more. Cool slightly, then purée in a food processor or blender. Reheat gently and season to taste with pepper.

Whisk in parsley and yogurt and heat for 30 seconds, without boiling, or yogurt will curdle. Serve immediately.

'One Cup' Haricot Bean and Ham Soup

Makes 8 servings

Here's where a food processor can really come in handy, reducing the preparation time to just a few minutes.

225g/8oz dried haricot beans,
  soaked (see page 80)
150g/5oz onion, **finely chopped**
150g/5oz carrot, **finely chopped**
150g/5oz celery, **finely chopped**
150g/5oz turnip, **finely chopped**

175g/6oz raw potatoes, **diced**
1 **bay leaf**
175g/6oz lean ham, **diced**
1 small **lettuce**
Pepper

Place beans and 2.25 litres/4 pints water in a large saucepan and bring to the boil. Reduce to a simmer and cook gently, partially covered, for 1½ hours or until beans are tender.

Add onion, carrot, celery, turnip, potato, and bay leaf, and simmer for 20 minutes more. Add ham and lettuce and simmer for 5 minutes; season to taste with pepper and serve.

Bean Vichyssoise

Makes 4 to 6 servings

The leeks, more than anything, give the characteristic flavour to a vichyssoise. Here, beans instead of potatoes give body and creaminess to the soup. Note that this tastes best when served chilled.

4 or 5 leeks	**250ml/8fl oz skimmed milk**
2 tablespoons olive oil	**2 tablespoons finely chopped**
450ml/¾ pint fat-free chicken	**spring onion or fresh chives**
stock or water	
One large tin cannellini beans	
in their liquid	

Cut 5cm/2in of dark green off the tops of the leeks and discard. Cut leeks in half vertically and wash them thoroughly. Cut into cross pieces about 2.5cm/1in thick.

In a medium saucepan heat oil. When hot, stir in leeks and sauté for 2 to 3 minutes. Add chicken stock or water, cover, and simmer for 10 minutes.

Uncover pan, add beans and their liquid. Cover and simmer gently for 10 minutes more. Purée in a food processor or blender. Return to pan. Stir in milk, heat until simmering, and serve garnished with spring onion or chives.

Black Bean Soup

Makes 6 servings

The first time I tried black beans was in a Cuban restaurant. I was surprised that instead of the refried-beans dish I expected I got a bowl of soup. But I surely wasn't disappointed! Here, too, you can make this a meal in itself by adding some diced low-fat ham. Serve with tortillas.

1 tablespoon olive oil
1 carrot, finely chopped
1 small onion, finely chopped
1 stalk celery, finely chopped
2×425g/15oz tins black beans
2 tablespoons lemon juice

1 teaspoon ground cumin
Tabasco
½ red pepper, finely chopped
1 spring onion, thinly sliced
2 tablespoons finely chopped
  coriander or parsley

In a medium saucepan heat olive oil and sauté the carrot, onion, and celery for about 5 minutes or until soft. If vegetables are sticking or begin to burn, add a few tablespoons of water and continue to cook.

Add beans and their liquid, lemon juice, cumin, and 1 litre/1¾ pints of water. Simmer for 30 minutes. Season to taste with Tabasco. Serve, garnished with some chopped pepper, spring onion, and coriander or parsley.

Black Bean and Onion Soup

Makes 6 servings

If you like onions you're going to love this soup. The red wine gives it a depth of flavour. If you have any left over, fill plastic drinking glasses and freeze for individual servings with sandwiches another time.

2 tablespoons corn oil
6 onions, thinly sliced
1 tablespoon sugar
250ml/8fl oz red wine

350g/12oz freshly cooked black
  beans or 425g/15oz tin
Pepper

In a large saucepan heat oil. Add onions, stir, and sauté for 5 minutes, stirring frequently. Add sugar and red wine; cover the pan and simmer, very gently for 20 minutes. Check the onions frequently to make sure they are not burning. If they begin to stick to the bottom of the pan, then simply add some water to loosen them.

Add beans and 900ml/1¾ pints water then cover, and simmer for 30 minutes longer. Season to taste with pepper.

Garbure: A French Soup of Beans and Cabbage

Makes 6 servings

Using the standard cooking methods, this soup must simmer for 1½ hours. With a pressure cooker, however, you can cut the time down to a mere 10 minutes at high pressure and another 10 minutes steeping before you open the pot. This is a real timesaver you'll appreciate having in your cooking repertoire.

225g/8oz haricot or cannellini beans, soaked (see page 80)
450g/1lb new potatoes, peeled and cut into 1cm/½in cubes
Two 397g/14oz tins no-salt added tomatoes

6 cloves garlic, cut into thin slivers
350g/12oz cabbage, shredded
½ teaspoon rosemary
Salt and pepper to taste

Place beans, potatoes, tomatoes, 750ml/1¼ pints water, garlic, cabbage, and rosemary in a large saucepan. Bring to the boil, cover, and simmer gently for 1½ hours, or until the beans are tender. Make sure the level of the liquid remains constant during the entire time the soup is simmering; replenish evaporated liquid with water.

Season to taste with salt and pepper.

Swedish Yellow Split Pea Soup

Makes 6 servings

Sweden's version of split pea soup has a distinctive taste you'll enjoy.

*200g/7oz yellow split peas,
  soaked (see page 80) and
  drained*
2 small onions, finely chopped
½ teaspoon thyme
*½ teaspoon powdered
  marjoram*

*2 whole cloves or ¼ teaspoon
  ground cloves*
*175g/6oz very lean bacon,
  finely chopped*
*6 tablespoons skimmed milk,
  optional*
Pepper

Place soaked split peas, onions, herbs, and cloves with 1.25 litres/2¼ pints water in a large saucepan. Bring to the boil and then simmer for 1 hour. Remove whole cloves and purée the mixture in a blender or food processor until smooth; return soup to the pan. Simmer with the bacon for 15 to 30 minutes or more. Add milk, if you wish, and season to taste with pepper.

Split Pea, Carrot, and Chicken Soup

Makes 8 servings

Why is it that chicken tastes so tender in soups in restaurants but tough when made at home? Because one tends to overcook the chicken. Like fish, chicken breast meat takes just a few minutes in a bubbling stock such as this one. All you need to complete the meal is some pasta.

200g/7oz split peas
½ teaspoon each garlic powder
* and ground cumin*
¼ teaspoon each powdered
* ginger and curry powder*
6 carrots, cut into 1cm/½ in
* rounds*

450g/1lb skinless, boneless
* chicken breasts cut into*
* 2.5cm/1 in cubes*
Pepper

Place peas, garlic, cumin, ginger, and curry powder in a medium saucepan. Add 1.25 litres/2¼ pints water and slowly bring to the boil. Reduce to a simmer, cover, and cook gently for 30 to 45 minutes.

Add carrots and cook for 15 minutes longer; add chicken and cook for 5 minutes or until chicken is just cooked through. Season to taste with pepper.

Split Pea and Potato Soup

Makes 8 servings

Who'd have thought that this traditional favourite had such cholesterol-lowering potential? Unfortunately most restaurants make it with a lot of pork fat. This healthy version can be made into a main course by adding diced low-fat bacon and serving with a chunk of crusty French bread. Because it takes a while to make, and freezes so beautifully, this recipe will give you enough to freeze for another evening.

450g/1lb split peas, picked over and rinsed
150g/5oz carrot, chopped
1 celery stalk, chopped
1 small onion, chopped
2 tablespoons tomato purée
¼ teaspoon garlic powder

½ teaspoon marjoram
1 bay leaf
2 medium potatoes
Pepper
2 tablespoons finely chopped fresh herbs, such as parsley, dill, and basil, optional

Place split peas in a large saucepan and cover with 2.25 litres/4 pints water. Slowly bring to a simmer and skim off foam that rises to the top. After all foam has been skimmed off, add carrots, celery, onion, tomato purée, garlic, marjoram, and bay leaf. Simmer, partially covered, for 45 minutes.

While soup is simmering, peel potatoes and cut into 1cm/½in cubes. After 45 minutes, add potatoes to the soup and continue to simmer, Uncovered, for 30 minutes more. Remove bay leaf and season with pepper. Stir in optional fresh herbs. Serve as it is or, with a wooden spoon, stir the soup quite vigorously to mash some of the peas into a purée to thicken the soup.

Three-Bean Soup with Celery and Lemon

Makes 4 to 6 servings

The Greeks like to add a squeeze of lemon to just about everything they eat. The citrus flavour with the beans is unusual and delicious. If you can't find one of the three beans, you can either substitute another type or use 340g/12oz each of just two kinds.

225g/8oz soaked or one small tin white beans, *such as* haricot *or* cannellini *drained*
225g/8oz soaked or one small tin butter beans, *drained*
225g/8oz soaked or one small tin chickpeas, *drained*

4 stalks celery, finely chopped
1 small onion, chopped
4 tablespoons lemon juice
Pepper
2 tablespoons finely chopped fresh herbs such as parsley or dill, for garnish

In a large saucepan, bring 900ml/2 pints water, along with the beans, and chickpeas, celery and onion, to the boil. Reduce to a simmer, and cook gently, partially covered, for 1½ hours if you are using dried and soaked beans or 45 minutes to 1 hour if you are using tinned beans.

When beans are soft, purée in a blender or food processor with lemon juice. Season to taste with pepper. Garnish, if you wish, with fresh herbs to liven up the colour.

White Bean Minestrone

Makes 6 servings

This classic soup is an Italian tradition. Serve with a meal of spaghetti and marinara sauce. A glass of Chianti complements this meal perfectly.

2 tablespoons olive oil
150g/5oz carrots, finely
 chopped
50g/2oz each onion and celery,
 finely chopped
150g/5oz haricot beans, soaked
 or 200g/7oz cooked white
 beans, drained and rinsed
397g/14oz tin no-salt added
 tomatoes
½ teaspoon dried oregano

350g/12oz raw white cabbage,
 shredded
175g/6oz potatoes, peeled and
 diced
350g/12oz courgettes, diced
Pepper
2 tablespoons finely chopped
 fresh parsley or basil,
 optional
4-6 tablespoons grated
 Parmesan, optional

In a large saucepan heat olive oil and sauté the carrots, onion, and celery for 2 minutes; stirring constantly. Add 1.25 litres/2¼ pints water, soaked dry beans, tomatoes, and oregano, and simmer for 1 hour. If you are using tinned beans, add them now along with the cabbage and potatoes, and simmer for 45 minutes.

Add courgette and simmer for 5 minutes only. Season to taste with pepper, and add parsley or basil and Parmesan, if you wish.

Hearty Chickpea Soup with Bacon

Makes 8 servings

This makes a hearty meal-in-a-bowl. As with any of the bean soups you can always substitute another kind of beans for the chickpeas. In fact, you can combine two, three, or more types for interesting flavour and appearance.

2 tablespoons olive oil
1 large onion, finely chopped
2 carrots, finely chopped
1 stalk celery, finely chopped
2 cloves garlic, crushed
397g/14oz tin no-salt added tomatoes
450g/1lb potatoes, cut into 2.5cm/1in cubes
½ teaspoon dried rosemary

425g/15oz cooked tinned chickpeas, drained and rinsed
350g/12oz Canadian cured lean bacon, cut into 1cm/½ in cubes
Pepper
4 tablespoons finely chopped fresh parsley or watercress leaves

In a large saucepan, heat olive oil and sauté onion, carrots, celery, and garlic for 2 minutes, stirring continuously.

Add tomatoes and 900ml/1½ pints water, and bring to the boil. Add potatoes and rosemary. Simmer for 30 minutes. Add chickpeas and bacon and simmer for 30 minutes more. Season to taste with pepper and garnish with parsley or watercress.

Portuguese Chickpea and Kale Soup

Makes 8 servings

The red wine vinegar really perks up the flavour of this soup the way salt would.

2 medium onions, chopped
4 tablespoons each chopped
 green pepper and celery
200g/7oz cooked or tinned
 chickpeas
225g/8oz turkey breast or lean
 smoked ham, cut into
 2cm/½ in cubes
2×397g/14oz tins tomatoes,
 no-salt added, coarsely
 chopped

1 bay leaf
450g/1lb curly kale
225g/8oz potatoes, unpeeled
 and cut into 1cm/½ in cubes
1 tablespoon red wine vinegar
Pepper

In a large saucepan, combine onions, pepper, and celery, along with chickpeas, turkey or ham, tomatoes, and 1.25 litres/2¼ pints water. Add the bay leaf and bring to the boil. Reduce heat and simmer, partially covered, for 1 hour.

Meanwhile, remove and discard the tough stems from the kale; wash the leaves and chop them. Add kale and potatoes to the soup and cook for 20 minutes more. Remove the bay leaf. Add the vinegar and plenty of pepper before serving.

Chicken and Bean Gumbo

Makes 8 servings

Depending on how spicy you like soup, you'll think this is either fiery or just right. If you have less than adventurous tastebuds, you may want to cut back on the cayenne and mixed herbs.

2 tablespoons olive oil
50g/2oz each finely-chopped
   onion, red pepper, and
   celery
25g/1oz oat bran
¼ to ½ teaspoon cayenne
½ teaspoon dried mixed herbs
½ teaspoon garlic powder
1.25 litres/2 ¼ pints fat-free
   chicken stock or water

1 bay leaf
675g/1 ½ lb red kidney beans,
   cooked, drained and rinsed
675g/1 ½ lb boneless, skinless
   chicken breasts or turkey
   breast meat, cut into
   2.5cm/1 in cubes

In a large saucepan, heat olive oil and sauté onion, pepper, and celery for 5 minutes, stirring continuously.

Add oat bran and flavourings and continue to sauté, stirring continuously, for 3 minutes or until oat bran begins to turn brown.

Add stock or water and bring to a simmer. Add bay leaf and beans and simmer, uncovered, for 25 minutes. Add cubed chicken and simmer for 5 minutes or until chicken is just cooked through. Remove bay leaf and serve immediately.

Southern Haricot Bean and Sweet Potato Soup

Makes 4 main-course servings

This is rich enough to serve as a meal, with only one saucepan to clean up. The sweetness of the beans and sweet potatoes contrasts well with the smoked bacon. Serve it with crusty French bread.

1 tablespoon olive oil
1 small onion, finely chopped
1 celery stalk, finely chopped
1 carrot, finely chopped
225g/8oz dried haricot beans, soaked (see page 80), or 425g/15oz tin, drained and rinsed

450g/1lb sweet potatoes, peeled and cut into 2.5cm/1in dice
225g/8oz smoked lean bacon, diced
⅛ teaspoon mace
¼ teaspoon grated orange zest
50g/2oz frozen peas, thawed
Pepper

In a large saucepan heat the oil and sauté the onion, celery, and carrot for 1 minute. Add 1.25 litres/2¼ pints water. Bring to the boil and add soaked dried beans, simmer them for 45 minutes before adding further ingredients. If you are using tinned beans, add them to the vegetables in the saucepan when the water comes to the boil

Add sweet potatoes, bacon, mace, and orange zest. Simmer, partially covered, for 30 minutes longer, or until the potatoes and beans are tender. Add peas and simmer 1 minute longer, then season with pepper to taste.

Pasta e Fagioli

Makes 6 servings

Nutritionists point to this classic dish, lovingly referred to by the old Italians as 'pasta fazool', as a wonderful example of how the amino acids of the beans and the pasta combine to form complete protein as high in quality as that from meat. And now we also know that the beans contribute to low cholesterol levels in those who enjoy them regularly.

2 tablespoons olive oil
1 small onion, finely chopped
½ carrot, finely chopped
½ celery stalk, finely chopped
1 clove garlic, crushed
225g/8oz tin no-salt added tomato sauce or tomatoes, chopped
½ teaspoon dried oregano
2 tablespoons chopped fresh basil, optional
450g/16oz tin cannellini beans, drained and rinsed
100g/4oz pasta, such as macaroni, penne, or rigatoni
Pepper

In a medium saucepan heat olive oil, then add onion, carrot, celery, and garlic, cover and sweat gently for 5 minutes. Stir once or twice, adding a tablespoon of water if vegetables are sticking, then cover and simmer for 5 minutes more or until vegetables are very tender.

Add tomato sauce and oregano (and basil if you have it) and simmer for 5 minutes. Add beans and simmer for 10 minutes. If you wish you can mash half of the beans against the sides of the pan to make the soup thicker. Add pasta and simmer for 10 minutes or until pasta is cooked and soup is quite thick. Season with pepper.

Provençal Bean and Garlic Soup

Makes 8 servings

Those who love it maintain that there may be too little garlic, enough garlic, but never too much garlic! This dish has enough, not too much, so don't cut back. And, to enjoy to its fullest, use fresh basil leaves if you can get them, dried basil just doesn't work here. This soup comes from the countryside of France—and they say French food isn't healthy!

1 tablespoon olive oil
1 onion, finely chopped
6 cloves garlic, crushed
3 carrots, finely chopped
1 stalk celery, finely chopped
397g/14oz tin no-salt added
*   tomatoes, chopped*
½ teaspoon dried thyme
225g/8oz dried haricot or
*   cannellini beans, soaked (see*
*   page 80) or 450g/16oz tin,*
*   drained*

4 tablespoons black olives,
*   chopped*
275g/10oz frozen green beans,
*   thawed*
2 tablespoons finely chopped
*   fresh basil leaves, optional*
Pepper

In a large saucepan heat olive oil, and sauté onion, garlic, carrots, and celery, for 3 minutes. Add 1.75 litres/3 pints water, tomatoes, thyme, and white beans.

Bring liquid to the boil, reduce to a simmer and partially cover. Cook over low heat, for 2 hours if you are using soaked dried beans or 30 minutes if you are using tinned beans.

Add black olives and green beans, and basil if desired, and simmer 30 minutes more. Season to taste with pepper and serve.

Indian Lentil Mulligatawny Soup

Makes 6 servings

If you've tried traditional mulligatawny soup at Indian restaurants you'll be delighted to have this dish frequently at home. Why not make a double batch and freeze half for another time?

1 tablespoon corn oil	*1 tablespoon curry powder*
1 carrot, finely chopped	*200g/7oz lentils*
1 onion, finely chopped	*225g/8oz tin no-salt added*
1 stalk celery, finely chopped	*tomatoes*
1 red pepper, finely chopped	**Pepper**

In a medium-sized saucepan, heat oil and sauté carrot, onion, celery, and red pepper for 2 to 3 minutes, stirring continuously.

Stir curry powder into the vegetables and sauté for 30 seconds. Add lentils, tomatoes, and 900ml/1½ pints water. Bring to the boil, reduce to a simmer, partially cover and cook gently, for 45 minutes or until lentils are very soft. Season with pepper.

Either purée first and then serve or serve straight from the pan.

Lentil, Potato, and Ham Soup

Makes 6 servings

Another example of a meal-in-a-bowl recipe that takes very little time and makes very little mess.

200g/7oz brown lentils
1 small onion, finely chopped
450g/1lb new potatoes, peeled
*   and cut into 1cm/½ in cubes*
4 spring onions, thinly sliced

175g/6oz lean ham, diced
1 tablespoon white wine
*   vinegar or lemon juice*
Pepper

In a large saucepan, bring 1.25 litres/2¼ pints water, lentils, onion, and potatoes to the boil. Reduce to a simmer, cover and cook gently for 25 minutes.

Add spring onions and ham and simmer 5 minutes more. Add vinegar and season to taste with pepper.

Turkey, Barley, and Lentil Soup

Makes 8 servings

This is a very hearty thick soup; one needs only a salad to round off the meal. Add some chopped fresh parsley at the end of the cooking time to provide colour. Make a double batch and freeze half for another time.

200g/7oz brown lentils
200g/7oz pearl barley
4 parsnips or carrots, peeled
*   and thinly sliced*
2 large cloves garlic, finely
*   chopped or 1 teaspoon garlic*
*   powder*
1½ teaspoons curry powder
2 tablespoons tomato purée

450g/1lb turkey breast meat,
*   cut into 2.5cm/1in cubes*
Pepper
50g/2oz fresh parsley or fresh
*   spinach leaves, finely*
*   chopped*
100ml/4fl oz low-fat yogurt,
*   optional*

In a large saucepan bring 3 litres/5 pints water to the boil, along with lentils, barley, parsnips, garlic, curry powder, and tomato purée. Reduce to a simmer and cook gently, uncovered for 45 minutes. If soup is too thick at that point add 250ml/8fl oz water and simmer for 5 minutes more.

Stir in meat and simmer 5 minutes more, or just enough to cook the turkey. Season to taste with pepper, and stir in parsley. If you wish, put a dollop of yogurt on each portion before serving.

Barley, Ham, and Carrot Soup

Makes 6 to 8 servings

I don't understand when people tell me they have no time to cook meals from scratch. This recipe is an excellent example of just how easy it can be to make a satisfying meal, with little time spent. Start the meal when you get home from work, then spend the next 45 minutes smelling the aroma while you relax from the day's labour. That's all there is to it. Serve with a crusty chunk of bread and, if you like, a glass of white wine.

1.75 litres/3 pints fat-free chicken stock or water
200g/7oz pearl barley
450g/1lb lean ham, cut into 1cm/½ in cubes

6 carrots, cut into 1cm/½ in rounds
1 onion, finely chopped
1 clove garlic, crushed
Pepper

In a large saucepan bring all the ingredients slowly to the boil. Skim off any froth that rises to the top. Cover and simmer gently for 45 minutes.

Scotch Broth

Makes 8 servings

This soup can be served before the main course or it can be the main course. Either way, it's hearty and comforting.

225g/8oz raw white cabbage,
   shredded
2 white turnips, peeled and cut
   into 2.5cm/1in dice
2 carrots, peeled and cut into
   2.5cm/1in rounds
1 tablespoon sugar
4 cloves garlic, crushed
150g/5oz pearl barley

900ml/1½ pints fat-free
   chicken stock or water
275g/10oz frozen peas, thawed
450g/1lb turkey breast, cut into
   2.5cm/1in cubes
Pepper
4 tablespoons finely chopped
   parsley or dill

In a large saucepan, place the cabbage, turnips, carrots, sugar, garlic, barley, and broth. Bring to the boil. Reduce to a simmer, cover, and cook gently for 1½ hours, adding water as liquid evaporates.

Add peas and turkey and simmer for 10 minutes more. Season to taste with pepper and scatter herbs on top.

Mushroom, Barley, and Haricot Bean Soup

Makes 8 servings

This is a terrific soup recipe just as it is. But you can make it into a main course by adding some shredded chicken breast meat and vegetables.

225g/8oz dried haricot beans,
   soaked (see page 80), or
   450g/1lb tinned beans,
   drained and rinsed
75g/3oz pearl barley
450g/1lb mushrooms, thinly
   sliced

1 teaspoon garlic powder
225g/8oz tin no-salt added
   tomato sauce
1.75 litres/3 pints fat-free
   chicken stock or water
Tabasco

Place all ingredients, except Tabasco, in a large saucepan. Slowly bring to the boil, and simmer, covered, for 2 hours, if you are using soaked dried beans, or for 1 hour if you are using tinned beans. If the level of liquid goes down, replace it with water or the soup will end up being too thick. Season to taste with Tabasco. This soup keeps on improving with each reheating.

Russian Beetroot and Barley Bortsch

Makes 6 to 8 servings

Regardless of what you think about *glasnost*, you're going to think this soup is the right step in culinary diplomacy. Just tasting this evokes in the imagination a picture of Russians gathered round the table on a cold winter's night enjoying their bortsch with a chunk of hearty bread. The vodka is optional.

*2×297/14oz tins no-salt added
   tomatoes
2 stalks celery, finely chopped
450g/1lb raw cabbage,
   shredded
1 onion, finely chopped
1 clove garlic, crushed
450g/1lb cooked beetroot,
   sliced*

*3 tablespoons red wine vinegar
1 tablespoon sugar
200g/7oz pearl barley
450g/1lb boneless chicken or
   turkey breast, finely diced
2 tablespoons finely chopped
   fresh parsley or dill
Pepper*

In a large saucepan, bring tomatoes, celery, cabbage, onion, garlic, beetroot, vinegar, sugar, and 1.15 litres/2 pints water to a simmer. Cover and cook gently for 30 minutes.

Add barley and simmer, covered, for 30 minutes more. Add chicken or turkey and parsley or dill, and simmer for 5 minutes. Season to taste with pepper.

Scottish Cock-a-Leekie Soup

Makes 4 servings

Another comfort soup, this has a very soothing quality to it.

450g/1lb leeks or onions   **50g/2oz** oat bran
900ml/1 ½ pints fat-free   **6 stoned prunes, cut in half**
   chicken stock or water   **250ml/8fl oz skimmed milk**
Pinch of allspice   **1 tablespoon chopped parsley**

Cut about 5cm/2in off the top dark green part of the leeks and discard. Cut leeks in half vertically and rinse them well under cold running water. Cut into 2.5cm/1in pieces.

Place leeks, chicken stock or water, allspice, oat bran and prunes in a medium saucepan and slowly bring to a simmer. Simmer, covered, for 30 minutes or until leeks are tender. Stir the bottom of the pan every now and then to make sure the oat bran is not sticking and burning.

Add milk and parsley and serve.

Greek-Style Chicken Lemon Soup

Makes 8 servings

Avgolemono soup, the classic chicken rice soup of Greece, gets its thick creaminess from egg yolks. Thanks to rice bran you can have the same rich consistency without the cholesterol, and get a soluble fibre boost to boot.

900ml/1 ½ pints fat-free   **225g/8oz chicken breast, cut**
   chicken stock   **into thin strips**
900ml/1 ½ pints water   **2 tablespoons chopped fresh**
50g/2 oz long-grain rice   **parsley**
25g/1oz rice bran   **2 spring onions, thinly sliced**
4 tablespoons lemon juice   **Pepper**

Place stock, water, rice, rice bran, and lemon juice in a large saucepan. Bring to the boil and simmer for 15 minutes or until rice is tender.

Stir soup well with a whisk, and add the chicken, parsley, and onions. Season to taste with pepper and simmer for 5 minutes more, or until the chicken is just tender.

Sweetcorn and Chilli Soup

Makes 10 servings

Did you know that chillies are an excellent source of vitamin C? In fact they're the main source of that vitamin for many Latin American people. Count on the apple fibre to thicken the soup and to supply some soluble fibre.

2 tablespoons corn or olive oil
1 onion, finely chopped
2 stalks celery, finely chopped
25g/1 oz apple fibre
750ml/1 ¼ pints tomato sauce
900ml/1 ½ pints fat-free
  chicken stock or water

225g/8oz green chillies,
  chopped
¼ teaspoon each cumin and
  chilli powders
275g/10oz sweetcorn kernels

In a medium-sized saucepan heat oil and sauté onion and celery for 5 minutes, stirring frequently. Add apple fibre, tomato sauce, chicken stock or water, chillies, cumin, chilli powder and sweetcorn. Bring to a simmer and cook gently for 10 minutes.

Cream of Cauliflower Soup

Makes 4 to 6 servings

Combine the red of the tomato with the white of the cauliflower and you
have a lovely pink soup, thickened by rice bran and flavoured with garlic.

450g/1lb cauliflower florets,	**1 teaspoon garlic powder**
frozen or fresh	**250ml/8fl oz skimmed milk**
25g/1oz *rice bran*	**Pepper**
2 tablespoons tomato purée or	**Finely chopped fresh parsley**
no-salt-added tomato sauce	**for garnish, optional**

In a medium-sized saucepan, cover cauliflower with 750ml/1¼
pints water and bring to the boil. Simmer, covered, for 10 to 20
minutes or until cauliflower is tender.

Drain cauliflower florets, reserving cooking liquid. Purée the
cauliflower in a blender or food processor with rice bran, tomato
purée, garlic, and milk. When nice and smooth, thin out with the
reserved cooking liquid.

Return soup to the heat and simmer for 5 minutes or until rice
bran has completely dissolved. Season with pepper to taste and
serve immediately, garnished, if you wish, with parsley.

Cream of Spinach Soup

Makes 4 servings

This soup has an elegant, gentle flavour, and the rice bran provides a
creamy texture. Low in fat, it is a nice alternative to salad.

1 tablespoon vegetable oil	**1 garlic clove, crushed**
1 small onion, finely chopped	**⅛ teaspoon ground nutmeg**
1 tablespoon *rice bran*	**100ml/4fl oz skimmed milk**
275g/10oz frozen chopped	**Pepper**
spinach, thawed, or 450g/1lb	
fresh spinach, washed,	
cooked, and chopped	

In a medium-sized saucepan, heat vegetable oil add onion and stir-fry for 30 seconds. Add 3 tablespoons water, cover, and simmer gently for 4 minutes, stirring every now and then to make sure the onion does not burn.

Uncover pan, add rice bran, and stir for 30 seconds. Add spinach, garlic, and 900ml/1½ pints water. Slowly bring to the boil; reduce to a simmer. Add nutmeg and cook gently, partially covered, for 25 minutes. Cool for 5 minutes, then purée in a blender or food processor with milk. Season to taste with pepper and serve.

Cream of Cabbage and Apple Soup

Makes 6 servings

The combination of cabbage and apple along with onion yields a flavour that's distinct from any of the three. The rice bran gives it a wonderful, creamy texture. It's also simple to prepare.

450g/1lb raw white cabbage,
   shredded
1 onion, thinly sliced
1 apple, peeled, cored, and
   chopped

1 tablespoons rice bran
Pepper

Simmer cabbage, onion, and apple in 1.25 litres/2¼ pints water, over low heat, covered, for 1 hour. Cool for 10 minutes.

Pour into blender or food processor, add rice bran, and blend for 1 minute or until smooth. Reheat and season to taste with pepper.

Chilled Tomato and Vegetable Soup

Makes 6 servings

50g/2oz rice bran
2 spring onions
1 red or green pepper, chopped
1 cucumber, peeled and
  chopped

3 tablespoons red wine vinegar
3×175ml/6fl oz V-8 juice
450ml/¾ pint tomato juice
¼ teaspoon garlic powder
Pepper

Purée all ingredients in a food processor or blender. Cover and chill, preferably overnight.

Salmon Chowder

Makes 6 to 8 servings

Like most people my age, I grew up thinking that fish was something that came only one way: fried and overdone. How wrong I was! Here's a nice way to get salmon, rich in protective oils, into the diet right along with the soluble fibre of beans.

2 tablespoons olive oil
1 onion, finely chopped
1 celery stalk, finely chopped
2 carrots, finely chopped
2 cloves garlic, crushed
900ml/1 ½ pints tomato juice
250ml/8fl oz Clamato juice
250ml/8fl oz white wine
1 bay leaf

275g/10oz cooked chickpeas *or*
  425g/15oz tin drained
275g/10oz frozen sweetcorn
  kernels
4 tablespoons finely chopped
  parsley
450g/1lb fillet of salmon *cut*
  into 2.5cm/1in chunks
Pepper

In a large saucepan heat olive oil and sauté onion, celery, carrots, and garlic for 5 minutes. Add tomato juice, Clamato juice, white wine, and bay leaf. Cover and simmer for 10 minutes.

  Add chickpeas, sweetcorn, parsley and salmon, and simmer for

5 minutes, or until salmon is just cooked through. Season to taste with pepper.

SALADS

Japanese Aduki Salad
Lentil and Cauliflower Salad
Italian Lentil and Parsley
  Salad
Barley Salad and Cucumbers
Carrot and Barley Salad
Three-Bean Salad
Black Bean, and Rice, and
  Green Pea Salad
Chickpea, Sweetcorn, and
  Pepper Salad
Chickpea and Four-Vegetable
  Salad
Black and White Bean Salad

Bean Waldorf Salad
Mackerel and Sweetcorn
  Salad
Mackerel and Bean Niçoise
  Salad
Pickled Sardine and Beetroot
  Salad
Spicy Rice, Ham, and Green
  Bean Salad
Rice Tabbouleh with Mint
  and Plum Tomatoes
Chickpea Russian Dressing
Creamy Cucumber Dressing

Japanese Aduki Salad

Makes 6 to 8 portions

If you have never tried aduki beans, you're in for a treat. This salad makes a terrific appetizer. How about serving it with teriyaki chicken or salmon?

225g/8oz aduki beans, *freshly*
  cooked
1 tablespoon sesame oil
1 tablespoon corn oil
3 tablespoons white wine
  vinegar
1 tablespoon soya sauce
⅛ teaspoon each grated lemon
  zest and powdered ginger

¼ teaspoon sugar
2 spring onions, thinly sliced
1 tablespoon sesame seeds,
  optional
Pepper
Lettuce leaves

Place beans in a mixing bowl. In another small mixing bowl, combine all remaining ingredients except lettuce and mix them well. Toss beans with this dressing, the cover the bowl and marinate for 2 hours at least or, preferably, overnight.

Serve the beans on lettuce leaves.

Lentil and Cauliflower Salad

Makes 6 servings

Here's just the dish to serve with chilled poached salmon—on a warm summer evening, perhaps, along with a glass of cold white wine.

200g/7oz lentils
1 cauliflower, cut into florets
4 tablespoons lime or lemon
  juice

4 tablespoons olive oil
4 tablespoons parsley, chopped
4 spring onions, thinly sliced
Pepper

Cook lentils in water to cover for 25 minutes or until just tender. Drain and cool under cold water; drain again.

Cook cauliflower for 5 minutes or until tender but still crisp. Break florets into even smaller pieces and combine them with lentils in a mixing bowl.

Combine lime or lemon juice, oil, parsley, and onions. Season to taste with pepper and combine with lentils and cauliflower. Cover and chill for 2 hours before serving.

Italian Lentil and Parsley Salad

Makes 6 servings

Here's a tasty way to add soluble fibre to the diet and have an alternative to the usual dinner salad at the same time. I like having this salad as an accompaniment to spaghetti and marinara sauce.

275g/10oz lentils
3 tomatoes
3 tablespoons olive oil
1 teaspoon Dijon mustard
2 tablespoons red wine vinegar

½ teaspoon dried oregano
4 tablespoons finely chopped
  parsley or basil
Pepper
Lettuce leaves

Cook lentils in 750ml/1¼ pints water, for 20 minutes or until just cooked through; take care not to overcook or they will become mushy. Drain and cool under running cold water.

Cut tomatoes in half and with a small spoon scoop out the seeds and discard. Dice the remaining tomato flesh.

Make a dressing of olive oil, mustard, vinegar, oregano, and parsley, and season to taste with pepper.

In a large mixing bowl toss lentils, tomatoes, and dressing, and chill for 30 minutes before serving on lettuce leaves.

Barley Salad and Cucumbers

Makes 6 servings

The very first time I had a cucumber salad as a child, it was served with fried chicken, and to this day I associate the two. But today I make an oven-fried chicken instead to cut down on fat, and I add barley to round out the salad.

200g/7oz cooked pearl barley
3 medium cucumbers, peeled and halved
4 tablespoons olive oil
3 tablespoons white wine vinegar

2 tablespoons fresh dill, finely chopped or 1 teaspoon dried dillweed
Freshly ground pepper

Place barley in a medium mixing bowl. With a small spoon, scrape out cucumber seeds and discard them. Chop cucumbers into dice and add to barley.

Mix together olive oil, vinegar, and dill. Add this to barley and cucumbers and toss well; season with pepper. Cover and chill in fridge for 1 hour, or overnight if you wish.

Carrot and Barley Salad

Makes 6 servings

A nice alternative to lettuce salads, this dish supplies soluble fibre by way of both the barley and carrots. The soft texture of the cooked barley and the crunchy uncooked vegetables provide a nice contrast I think you'll enjoy.

200g/7oz pearl barley
2 carrots, peeled and grated
1 celery stalk, grated
2 radishes, thinly sliced
2 spring onions, finely sliced

2 tablespoons olive oil
3 tablespoons lemon juice
Pepper
Shredded lettuce or cabbage

Cook barley in 900ml/1½ pints water, partially covered, for 25 minutes, or until just tender. Drain and cool to room temperature. Blend with carrots, celery, radishes, onions, olive oil, and lemon juice; season to taste with pepper. Serve on shredded lettuce or cabbage.

Three-Bean Salad

Makes 6 to 8 servings

What would a buffet be without three-bean salad? And no cookbook focusing on the foods that lower cholesterol would be complete without a good recipe for this soluble-fibre-packed dish. Not planning a buffet? Keep a container filled with the salad to enjoy with your sandwich at lunch.

275g/10oz cooked kidney beans *or drained and rinsed tinned beans*

275g/10oz cooked haricot, or *cannellini beans, or drained and rinsed tinned beans*

275g/10oz frozen green beans, thawed

Small jar cocktail onions, chopped

4 tablespoons chopped mixed pickles

3 tablespoons olive oil

2 teaspoons Dijon mustard

3 tablespoons red wine vinegar

½ teaspoon sugar

Pepper

Place red, white, and green beans in a mixing bowl. Stir in the cocktail onions and pickles.

In another small mixing bowl make a dressing out of olive oil, mustard, vinegar, sugar, and pepper. Toss the dressing with beans. Cover and chill for 1 hour before serving to allow the flavours to amalgamate and mellow.

Black Bean, Rice, and Green Pea Salad

Makes 6 servings

This salad creates a rainbow of colours. Serve it on crisp lettuce leaves.

350g/12oz cooked long-grain rice
275g/10oz frozen petit pois, thawed
275g/10oz cooked or drained and rinsed tinned black beans
2 tablespoons olive oil

2 tablespoons chopped red pepper
1 teaspoon Dijon mustard
3 tablespoons tomato sauce
3 tablespoons red wine vinegar
Pepper
Lettuce leaves

Place rice, peas, and black beans in a mixing bowl.

In a blender or food processor combine olive oil, red pepper, mustard, ketchup, and vinegar, and season to taste with pepper. Toss this dressing with the rice and beans. Chill, covered, for 2 hours. Serve on lettuce leaves.

Chickpea, Sweetcorn, and Pepper Salad

Makes 6 servings

An attractive and colourful dish, this can be made as spicy as you like with Tabasco. Along with a turkey sandwich it makes a nice summer's evening meal.

450g/1lb cooked or drained and rinsed tinned chickpeas
275g/10oz frozen sweetcorn kernels, thawed
1 green pepper, chopped

50g/2oz fresh parsley
3 tablespoons olive oil
3 tablespoons wine vinegar
Tabasco, optional
Lettuce leaves

In a mixing bowl, toss together chickpeas and sweetcorn. In a blender or food processor blend pepper, parsley, oil, vinegar, and Tabasco until smooth. Toss with chickpeas and sweetcorn. Cover and leave to stand for 1 hour if you wish to let chickpeas absorb the flavours of the dressing. Serve on lettuce leaves.

Chickpea and Four-Vegetable Salad

Makes 4 servings

It takes so little time, yet makes such a difference, to prepare a really worthwhile salad. When salad consists of nothing but lettuce and a chunk of tomato or two with bottled dressing, I can understand why people get sick of it. Here's an example of how a variety of vegetables can be combined to make a special salad. But don't stop here—create your own combinations.

2 tomatoes, cut in half
   horizontally
2 carrots, finely chopped
2 stalks celery, finely chopped
1 green pepper, seeds and
   membranes removed, finely
   chopped
275g/10oz cooked or drained
   and rinsed tinned chickpeas

2 tablespoons olive oil
4 tablespoons lemon or lime
   juice
1 teaspoon Dijon mustard
1 teaspoon dried mint
½ teaspoon honey
Pepper
Lettuce leaves or watercress

With a spoon, remove seeds from each of the tomato halves, then cut them into small dice.

In a large mixing bowl combine the tomatoes with other vegetables and chickpeas.

In a small bowl, combine oil, lemon juice, mustard, mint, and honey to make a dressing, and pour over chickpeas and vegetables. Toss well and season to taste with pepper. Cover and chill 1 hour before serving lettuce leaves or watercress.

Black and White Bean Salad

Makes 6 servings

Marinating the beans gives them a full flavour, but if you don't have the time you can skip that step. You can also mix the two beans together rather than keeping them separate, but they're more attractive in distinct mounds on the plate.

275g/10oz cooked black beans
275g/10oz cooked or drained
and rinsed tinned white
beans
1 red pepper, cut into
1cm/½ in cubes
1 small onion, finely sliced

1 clove garlic or ¼ teaspoon
garlic powder
6 tablespoons white wine
vinegar
1 teaspoon paprika
1 teaspoon chilli powder
2 tablespoons vegetable oil

Place black and white beans in separate bowls.

In a blender or food processor, combine pepper, onion, garlic, vinegar, paprika, chilli powder, and oil. Purée the sauce until smooth. Toss each batch of beans with 100ml/4fl oz of the sauce. Cover and marinate at room temperature for at least 30 minutes or up to 2 hours.

To serve, put each batch of beans, separately, on the side of a plate, leaving some room in the middle into which you can pour the remaining sauce.

Bean Waldorf Salad

Makes 4 to 6 servings

Why not stage a revival of this wonderful classic, updated with the soluble fibre of chickpeas or beans?

275g/10oz cooked or drained
and rinsed tinned chickpeas
or other white beans
2 Red Delicious apples, cored,
unpeeled, and diced into
1cm/½ in cubes

100g/4oz celery, diced
50g/2oz walnuts, chopped
3 tablespoons reduced-calorie
mayonnaise
2 tablespoons lemon juice
Lettuce

Place all ingredients, except lettuce, in a mixing bowl and toss well. Cover and chill for 2 hours before serving on a bed of lettuce.

Mackerel and Sweetcorn Salad

Makes 6 main-course servings

Decisions, decisions. Should you stick with the mackerel in this recipe or substitute salmon? Should you eat the salad on lettuce, or in a sandwich? Whatever your decisions, the recipe is delicious and you'll really enjoy it.

675g/1 ½ lb smoked mackerel, skinned, boned and diced
275g/10oz frozen sweetcorn kernels, thawed
1 large red pepper, finely chopped
150ml/5fl oz reduced-calorie mayonnaise
4 tablespoons lime or lemon juice
2 tablespoons finely chopped coriander
Shredded iceberg lettuce
Tomato quarters

In a mixing bowl, toss together mackerel, sweetcorn, and red pepper. In another bowl, mix mayonnaise with lime juice and coriander. Add this to the mackerel and mix well.

Chill, covered, for 2 hours. Serve on iceberg lettuce and garnish with tomato quarters.

Mackerel and Bean Niçoise Salad

Makes 6 to 8 servings

Summertime and the livin' is easy—just the time for a light main-course salad like this one. You can substitute salmon for the mackerel. I like this with sourdough rye bread, and a glass of Chardonnay wine to toast the sunset.

350g/12oz cooked mackerel,
   diced
450g/1lb tin cannellini beans,
   drained and rinsed
175g/6oz green beans, freshly
   cooked or frozen and thawed
2 tomatoes, cut into 2.5cm/1in
   dice
1 cucumber, peeled and cut
   into 2.5cm/1in dice

2 tablespoons capers
¼ teaspoon garlic powder
½ teaspoon Dijon mustard
2 tablespoons olive oil
3 tablespoons lemon juice
Pepper
Lettuce

In a bowl, combine mackerel, beans, green beans, tomatoes, and cucumber, and toss.

In a small bowl, combine capers, garlic powder, mustard, olive oil, and lemon juice to make a dressing and mix well; season to taste with pepper. Stir the dressing into the mackerel-and-bean mixture and toss well. Cover and chill for 1 to 2 hours before serving. Serve on a bed of lettuce.

Pickled Sardine and Beetroot Salad

Makes 4 to 6 servings

This certainly isn't a dish for everyone, but if you happen to be a sardine lover, you'll find it a great lunch along with a piece of crusty sourdough rye bread. If you don't like sardines, try the same recipe with tinned salmon. Both fish supply the EPA fish oils that protect against heart disease.

*4×120g/4oz tins sardines,
   packed in water, drained*
*350g/12oz, cooked beetroot,
   sliced*
24 cocktail onions, halved
*2 tablespoons mixed pickles,
   finely chopped*

2 teaspoons prepared mustard
*2 tablespoons reduced calorie
   mayonnaise or yogurt*
Lettuce leaves
*2 tablespoons finely chopped
   dill or parsley*

Empty sardines into a mixing bowl and break up.

Cut beetroot into small cubes and add to sardines. Add cocktail onions and pickles.

In a small bowl make a dressing of the mustard and mayonnaise; if too thick, thin with some juice from the cocktail onions or pickles. Toss with sardines and beetroot; chill for 1 hour. Serve on lettuce leaves and garnish with chopped herbs.

Spicy Rice, Ham, and Green Bean Salad

Makes 6 servings

I like to prepare salads such as this one early in the morning before starting the day's work, so it's ready later in the day for lunch. You can add the rice bran during preparation and it will sort of 'disappear' into the salad, or you can sprinkle it on at the last minute to give the salad a little crunchiness.

350g/12oz cooked long-grain   *4 tablespoons chilli sauce*
  rice   *3 tablespoons red wine vinegar*
275g/10oz green beans, cooked   *Pepper*
  and cut into 5cm/2in lengths *½ cup rice bran*
225g/8oz fat-free smoked ham, *Lettuce leaves*
  diced

Place rice in a mixing bowl and toss with green beans and ham.

In a blender or food processor combine chilli sauce and vinegar, and season to taste with pepper. Toss this dressing with the rice. Chill, covered, for 2 hours.

Just before serving, in order not to lose its special crunch, toss the salad with rice bran and serve on lettuce leaves.

Rice Tabbouleh with Mint and Plum Tomatoes

Makes 6 servings

One taste of this slightly modified Middle Eastern dish and you can almost see the minarets on the skyline. We've replaced the usual bulgar wheat with rice, but you can switch back to make the dish more authentic if you wish.

350g/12oz cooked long-grain rice
100g/4oz parsley, finely chopped
25g/1oz rice bran
6 spring onions, finely sliced
4 tablespoons fresh mint, chopped or 2 tablespoons dried mint

½ teaspoon grated lemon zest
4 tablespoons olive oil
3 tablespoons lemon juice
Pepper to taste
2 plum tomatoes, cut into 1cm/½ in dice
Lettuce leaves

Place rice in a mixing bowl.

In a blender or food processor combine all remaining ingredients, except tomatoes and lettuce. Blend until smooth; if too thick, thin with water. Toss this dressing with the rice. Chill, covered, for 2 hours. Just before serving, stir in the tomatoes and serve on lettuce leaves.

Chickpea Russian Dressing

Makes about 450ml/¾ pint

Now even your salad dressing can be a source of soluble fibre. Enjoy with cold meats and chilled poached salmon in addition to salads. The chickpeas add extra body to the dressing when blended smooth.

*150g/5oz tinned or freshly
  cooked chickpeas*
*4 tablespoons reduced-calorie
  mayonnaise*
3 tablespoons ketchup

*Small jar cocktail onions and
  their juice*
1 tablespoon Dijon mustard
3 tablespoons lemon juice
Pepper

Blend all ingredients until smooth and chill, covered, for 2 hours before serving.

Creamy Cucumber Dressing

Makes about 450ml/¾ pint

This dressing is delicious served over felafel (see page 141 for recipe).

*250ml/8fl oz plain low-fat
  yogurt*
*½ medium cucumber, finely
  chopped*
*1 teaspoon fresh-squeezed
  lemon juice*

1 clove garlic, crushed
½ teaspoon salt
*½ teaspoon ground white
  pepper*

Blend ingredients together in a jar and store in the fridge. Use generously with felafel as well as with fresh green salads.

VEGETARIAN ENTRÉES

Green Peppers Stuffed with Barley and Raisins
Black Bean Soufflés
Bean Mini Pizzas
Creole Red Bean Burgers
White Bean and Broccoli Stew
Lentil Burgers
Black Bean Chilli
Felafel
Barley, Split Pea, and Vegetable Stew
Vegetable, Bean, and Lentil Stew
Carrot and Kidney-Bean Loaf
Middle Eastern Barley, Lentil, and Rice Casserole
Greek Pastitsio with Lentils
Black-eyed Beans and Macaroni
Bean and Aubergine Curry
Hoppin' John
Bean Enchiladas
Indian Chickpea and Rice Biriyani
Barley, Pepper, and Bean-Curd Sauté
Tortilla and Black Bean Torte

Green Peppers Stuffed with Barley and Raisins

Makes 6 stuffed peppers

Stuffed peppers are usually a high-fat dish, made with greasy minced beef. This is a delightful alternative. You can add meat to this recipe by browning some very lean minced beef along with the onions and chopped peppers. Both versions taste great.

200g/7oz pearl barley
6 medium green or red peppers
1 tablespoon oil
1 small onion, chopped
100g/4oz raisins

2 tablespoons chopped fresh
* mint or 2 teaspoons dried*
¾ teaspoon ground cinnamon
2 tablespoons lemon juice
Pepper

Cook barley in about 1.25 litres/2¼ pints boiling water for 30 minutes; it should be tender but still have some bite to it. Drain and reserve for later.

Preheat oven to 180°C/350°F/gas mark 4.

Cut 1cm/½in slice off stem end of each pepper.

Discard stem but chop up what pepper remains and reserve for later. Empty peppers of seeds and ribs.

Over medium heat, in a large frying pan, preferably nonstick, heat the oil. Add onions and reserved chopped peppers. Stir-fry for a couple of minutes. Add 100ml/4fl oz water to the pan, cover, and simmer over low heat for 10 minutes, or until vegetables are tender.

Add to the pan the cooked barley, raisins, mint, cinnamon, and lemon juice. Stir around for a minute or so and remove from heat. Season to taste with pepper.

Scoop the barley mixture into the hollowed-out pepper cases. Fit the peppers into a baking dish so that the peppers touch and help support each other. Add about 2.5cm/1in water to the pan, cover, and bake for 45 minutes to 1 hour or until tender.

Black Bean Soufflés

Makes 6 servings

You'll have a hard time deciding whether to serve this as a side dish or the entrée. Either way it's delicious and nutritious, supplying ingredients from all four food groups. I think this will become one of your favourites.

450g/1lb cooked black beans
50g/2oz oat bran
100g/4oz green chillies, chopped
250ml/8fl oz tomato sauce
1 jalapeño pepper, finely
  chopped, optional

½ teaspoon each ground
  cumin and garlic powder
2 tablespoons lemon juice
50g/2oz low fat Cheddar cheese
4 egg whites
1 spring onion, thinly sliced

Preheat oven to 200°C/400°F/gas mark 6.

With an electric mixer, food processor, or blender purée all ingredients, except egg whites and spring onion.

Beat egg whites until stiff, then fold these into the purée. Spoon the mixture into 6 ramekins and bake for 20 minutes. Sprinkle spring onion over the tops and serve immediately.

Bean Mini Pizzas

Makes 4 servings

'And now for something completely different!' Who needs pepperoni when you have toppings like this? Serve with a salad with Italian dressing or a simple olive-oil vinaigrette and you're all set. A nice Italian red wine complements the meal perfectly.

4 muffins, split in half
250ml/8fl oz no-salt-added
 tomato sauce
2 tablespoons apple fibre

450g/1lb cooked black beans
Barbecue seasoning, to taste
100g/4oz low-fat cheese, grated

Lightly toast muffins and set on one side.

In a small saucepan simmer tomato sauce and apple fibre for 2 minutes; set aside.

With an electric mixer or in a food processor, purée black beans and barbecue seasoning.

Preheat the grill. To assemble the mini pizzas, spoon 1 tablespoon of tomato sauce onto each muffin, top with 3 tablespoons bean mixture, then top that with 1 more tablespoon of tomato sauce and sprinkle cheese on top. Grill for 1 minute or until cheese topping begins to brown.

Creole Red Bean Burgers

Makes twelve burgers

The recipe calls for blending the beans and seasonings till smooth and shaping into burgers. If you want additional texture, try chopping the beans instead. In either case, serve the burgers on buns with onion rings, lettuce, and tomato slices with ketchup or mustard.

450g/16oz cooked or drained and rinsed tinned red beans	**¼ teaspoon cayenne**
4 onions, thinly sliced	**Tabasco to taste**
½ red pepper, chopped	**½ teaspoon thyme**
4 tablespoons chopped fresh parsley	**¼ teaspoon garlic powder**
	6 tablespoons apple fibre

In a food processor or blender, combine beans, onions, red pepper, parsley, cayenne, Tabasco, thyme, garlic powder, and 2 tablespoons apple fibre. Process until smooth.

Place remaining apple fibre in a shallow bowl. Dipping your hands in the apple fibre, shape the bean purée into burgers about 5cm/2in in diameter and 1cm/½in thick.

Cook burgers for 5 minutes on each side in a non-stick frying pan.

White Bean and Broccoli Stew

Makes 6 servings

Mint gives this Middle Eastern food its characteristic flavour. You can use all one type of bean, but for more pizzazz use a mixture of three different kinds of white bean.

2 tablespoons olive oil
1 onion, finely chopped
2 red or green peppers, seeds and membranes removed, thinly sliced
225g/8oz mushrooms, thinly sliced
1 tablespoon fresh or 2 teaspoons dried mint

150g/5oz each of cooked or tinned white *haricot, kidney,* or *cannellini* beans, drained and rinsed
275g/10oz broccoli florets
Pepper or Tabasco

In a medium-sized saucepan heat olive oil and sauté onion and peppers for 5 minutes, stirring constantly. If vegetables begin to brown too quickly or stick to the saucepan, add a few tablespoons of water.

Add mushrooms and mint, cover and simmer for 5 minutes; add beans and simmer for 10 minutes. Add broccoli, 250ml/8fl oz water, cover and simmer 5 minutes, or until broccoli is just tender; season to taste with pepper.

Lentil Burgers

Makes eight 7.5cm/3in burgers

This dish comes absolutely packed with soluble fibre, from both the lentils and the rice bran. In fact, it has as much soluble fibre as 150g/5oz of oat bran. If you missed having oat-bran muffins or cereal for breakfast, you can get your day's supply of soluble fibre at lunch. Serve the burgers on buns or muffins.

200g/7oz lentils	*½ teaspoon garlic powder*
1 tablespoon olive oil	*25g/1oz rice bran*
1 small onion, chopped	*2 tablespoons ketchup*
150g/5oz carrots, chopped	*Pepper*
1 egg white	*Chopped parsley for garnish*

Bring 450ml/¾ pint water to the boil, add lentils, cover, and simmer gently for 25 minutes or until lentils are just done; you don't want them too mushy. Drain through a sieve and keep them in the sieve for about 1 hour or until all the water drains away.

In a small frying pan heat olive oil, add onions and carrots and stir-fry for 1 minute. Add some water to the frying pan, cover, and simmer for 10 minutes or until the vegetables are tender.

In a food processor or blender, mix the lentils, vegetables, egg white, garlic powder, half the rice bran, ketchup and pepper to taste.

Just before cooking, put remaining rice bran in shallow dish. Shape the mixture into 8 burgers about 7.5cm/3in in diameter. Coat each burger with the rice bran. In a nonstick frying pan, sauté over medium-high heat, for about 4 minutes, on one side. With a spatula, carefully turn burgers over and cook for 3 minutes on the second side. Sprinkle parsley on top and serve.

Black Bean Chilli

Makes 6 servings

The word 'chilli' refers, of course, to chilli peppers, from which the flavour of this dish originates. Original chilli recipes used no beans at all—just meat and chilli peppers. Today the emphasis is on the beans. This recipe calls for no meat at all, but you can add some browned very-lean minced beef or turkey breast. Or you can add cooked macaroni to make what we term 'chilli mac' in our house.

2 red peppers, thinly sliced
1 tablespoon olive oil
1 tablespoon each chilli powder
*   and ground cumin*
½ teaspoon garlic powder
675g/1 ½ lb cooked black beans
250ml/8fl oz bean cooking
*   liquid*
3 tablespoons ketchup

OPTIONAL ACCOMPANIMENTS
4 tablespoons chopped
*   coriander*
2 tablespoons spring onion
Low-fat yogurt
100g/4oz low-fat Cheddar
*   cheese, grated*

In a medium saucepan, sauté red peppers in olive oil for 2 minutes. Cover and simmer for 5 to 10 minutes or until soft; if peppers stick to the saucepan, add a tablespoon or two of cold water.

Stir chilli powder and cumin into the peppers and stir-fry for 30 seconds. Add garlic powder and black beans with their liquid. Simmer, covered, for 30 minutes. Uncover and add ketchup. If chilli is too soupy, simmer for 15 minutes more uncovered.

Serve with optional accompaniments.

Felafel

Makes eighteen 2.5cm/1in balls

Felafel is the original vegetable burger, served throughout the Middle East. Instead of the traditional deep-frying, this recipe cuts the fat content by baking. Serve the burgers in pitta pockets with chopped tomatoes, lettuce, and Creamy Cucumber Dressing.

275g/10oz cooked chickpeas or black-eyed peas
15g/½ oz rice bran, finely ground
2 cloves fresh garlic, crushed
½ teaspoon ground coriander
1 teaspoon ground cumin
¼ teaspoon cayenne

1 teaspoon dried or 2 tablespoons chopped coriander
Pepper
Flour
Creamy Cucumber Dressing (see page 132)

In a food processor or blender combine all ingredients, except flour. The purée will not be entirely smooth, which is good.

Preheat oven to 180°C/350°F/gas mark 4.

Dipping your hands lightly in flour, if you need to, shape the purée into balls, about 2.5cm/1in in diameter. Lightly grease a large frying pan and heat until very hot. Sauté the balls on all sides, then transfer them to a baking pan and bake for 30 minutes. Serve with Creamy Cucumber Dressing.

Barley, Split Pea, and Vegetable Stew

Makes 6 servings

This stew is thick with ingredients and flavour, rich in soluble fibre, and bursting with colour. You may also wish to add chicken, cubes of very lean beef, or fish. If you opt for the fish, add whatever amount you wish during the last 10 minutes of simmering.

90g/3 ½ oz pearl barley
90g/3 ½ oz green split peas
1 small onion, finely chopped
1 clove garlic, crushed
397g/14oz tin no-salt-added
  tomatoes
½ teaspoon celery seed

2 carrots, finely chopped
150g/5oz fresh or frozen green
  beans, cut into 2.5cm/1in
  lengths
150g/5oz sweetcorn kernels
1-2 tablespoons lemon juice
Pepper

Bring barley, peas, onion, garlic, 750ml/1¼ pints water, and tomatoes to the boil. Add celery seed, cover, and simmer gently for 45 minutes.

Add carrots and green beans if you are using fresh ones, cover again, and simmer 15 minutes longer. Uncover, add sweetcorn and frozen green beans if you are using them. Simmer, uncovered, for 10 to 15 minutes or until the juices have been almost entirely absorbed by the barley and split peas. Season to taste with lemon juice and pepper.

Vegetable, Bean, and Lentil Stew

Makes 8 servings

90g/3 ½ oz lentils
90g/3 ½ oz split green peas
397g/14oz tin no-salt-added
   tomatoes
1 small onion, finely chopped
1 green pepper, finely chopped

1 carrot, finely chopped
1 stalk celery, finely chopped
450g/16oz cooked red kidney
   beans
275g/10oz sweetcorn kernels
Pepper

In a large saucepan bring to the boil lentils, split peas, tomatoes, onions, peppers, carrot, celery, and 450ml/¾ pint water. Simmer, covered, for 25 minutes.

Add beans and sweetcorn. If needed, add some water to just cover mixture. Cover and simmer for 15 minutes more or until lentils and peas are cooked through and tender; season to taste with pepper and serve.

Carrot and Kidney-Bean Loaf

Makes about 6 to 8 servings

The colour and texture of this dish make it an attractive and satisfying main course. The tastes of carrot and bean play off each other very well.

1 tablespoon corn oil	**½ teaspoon thyme**
1 onion, thinly sliced	**Pinch allspice**
3 carrots, grated	**Pepper**
550g/1 ¼ lb freshly cooked or	**2 egg whites**
drained and rinsed tinned	**Tomato sauce (see page 233),**
red kidney beans	**optional**

Preheat oven to 180°C/350°F/gas mark 4.

In a large frying pan heat oil, add onion and stir-fry for 1 or 2 minutes. Add a tablespoon of water and cook for another 2 minutes or until the onion begins to soften.

Add the grated carrots and cook, stirring frequently, for about 2 minutes or until they just begin to wilt. Do not overcook because you want to preserve some of their crunch to give texture to the bean loaf.

Put half the beans with the onions and carrots in the bowl of a food processor or in a blender. Process with spices and egg whites. In a mixing bowl, toss this bean paste with the remaining whole beans.

Spoon the mixture into a loaf tin about 20×10cm/8×4in and bake for 45 minutes. Remove from oven and leave for 15 minutes. Spoon the servings out of the loaf tin and serve, if you wish, with tomato sauce.

Middle Eastern Barley, Lentil, and Rice Casserole

Makes 6 to 8 servings

You'll find the combination of apricots and raisins along with the lentils and barley in this dish to be exciting, with just a touch of sweetness. Enjoy with toasted pitta bread.

1 tablespoon olive oil
1 small onion, finely chopped
2 cloves garlic, crushed
1 teaspoon ground cinnamon
1 teaspoon sugar
90g/3 ½ oz lentils
90g/3 ½ oz pearl barley

90g/3 ½ oz long-grain rice
40g/1 ½ oz dried apricots, chopped
65g/2 ½ oz raisins
1 ½ teaspoons dried mint
Pepper

In a large saucepan heat oil and sauté onion and garlic for 2 minutes. Stir in cinnamon and sugar, then add 900ml/1½ pints water. Add lentils and barley. Cover and simmer gently for 20 minutes.

Add rice, apricots, raisins, and mint. Stir ingredients together, cover the pan again, and simmer for 20 minutes more or until all ingredients are tender and have absorbed the liquid. Season to taste with pepper.

Greek Pastitsio with Lentils

Makes 8 servings

The traditional pastitsio comes with more than its share of saturated fat. Even the Greeks eat that dish just once in a while. Here's a way to make it positively healthy.

225g/8oz macaroni	*225g/8oz no-salt-added tomato*
200g/7oz lentils	*sauce*
1 tablespoon corn oil	*250ml/8fl oz skimmed milk*
1 small onion, finely chopped	*2 tablespoons* oat bran
3 tablespoons white wine	*Pinch nutmeg*
½ teaspoon ground cinnamon	*50g/2oz low-fat cheese, grated*

Cook macaroni in boiling water for about 10 minutes and drain; cool under cold running water and reserve for later. Cook lentils in 900ml/1½ pints boiling water for about 25 minutes or until tender. Drain.

Preheat oven to 180°C/350°F/gas mark 4.

In a large frying pan, heat oil and sauté onion for 2 minutes. Add wine and simmer for 10 minutes or until wine has evaporated and onion is tender. Add cinnamon, tomato sauce, and lentils; simmer for 3 to 4 minutes.

In a medium-sized saucepan, heat milk. Whisk in oat bran and nutmeg and simmer for 1 minute, stirring constantly; remove from heat. Stir macaroni into milk and mix well.

Spoon half of the macaroni in the bottom of a 23cm/9in square baking tin. Spoon half of the lentil mixture on top and spread evenly. Repeat with remaining macaroni and lentils. Sprinkle on cheese. Cover with foil and bake for 15 minutes or until casserole is hot.

Black-Eyed Beans and Macaroni

Makes 6 to 8 servings

Black-eyed beans have more soluble fibre than any of the other dried beans or peas. You can also use this southern favourite in a number of the recipes in this book.

225g/8oz black-eyed beans   **Pinch nutmeg**
225g/8oz macaroni   **Pepper**
350ml/12fl oz skimmed milk   *40g/1 ½ oz* **Parmesan**
25g/1oz oat bran

Cook black-eyed beans in 900ml/1½ pints water, covered, for 45 minutes or until tender; drain.

Cook macaroni in boiling water for about 10 minutes. Drain and refresh under cold water.

Bring milk, oat bran, nutmeg, and pepper slowly to a simmer, whisking constantly so that oat bran does not burn. Cook gently for 2 minutes. Add black-eyed beans, macaroni, and cheese to sauce, and simmer, mixing thoroughly, for 2 minutes or until everything is hot throughout.

Bean and Aubergine Curry

Makes 4 servings

I find aubergine a bit on the mushy side when used as the main ingredient. Yet I love the way it absorbs flavours such as curry. In this dish, the combination of the aubergine and the beans works beautifully. Served over rice, this makes a very satisfying meal, with or without meat. You might also consider including 225g/8oz of very lean browned minced beef at the end of the recipe to satisfy any carnivorous cravings.

225g/8oz dried white beans, such as haricot, or kidney, soaked (see page 80), or 275g/10oz tinned white beans
450g/1lb aubergine, cut into 2.5cm/1in pieces

2 carrots, peeled and cut into 1cm/½ in rounds
1 onion, thinly sliced
2 teaspoons curry powder
1 teaspoon ground cumin
1 tablespoon lemon juice
Pepper

Place all ingredients except lemon juice and pepper in a large saucepan. If you are using dried beans, add just enough water to cover the beans. Cover and cook slowly for 1½ to 2 hours or until beans are tender and vegetables are cooked. While beans are simmering, check them every now and then to make sure they are always just covered with liquid, or they will not soften.

If you are using tinned beans, place all ingredients, including liquid from beans in a large saucepan. Add 100ml/4fl oz water, cover and simmer gently for 45 minutes or until aubergine is tender.

Drain beans and aubergine, and place in a clean saucepan, reserving liquid. Place cooking liquid in a large frying pan and boil it until you have only 100ml/4fl oz left. Stir this liquid and lemon juice into the stew and season to taste with pepper.

Hoppin' John

Makes 6 servings

Instead of the usual sandwich for lunch, try this dish on lettuce leaves with some chopped tomatoes. Spoon a low-fat dressing over it and serve with fresh bread.

225g/8oz black-eyed beans
1 small onion, finely chopped
½ teaspoon cayenne
75g/3oz very lean ham,
* chopped*

1 bay leaf
200g/7oz long-grain rice

In a medium-sized saucepan simmer black-eyed beans, onion, cayenne, ham, bay leaf, and water to cover for 45 minutes or until black-eyed beans are soft.

Add rice, cover, and simmer for 15 minutes, or until rice is soft and has absorbed liquid. Remove bay leaf and serve.

Bean Enchiladas

Makes 6 servings

While preparing these enchiladas, try making some tortilla chips to dip in salsa while waiting for the main course. Just take some tortillas, cut them into wedges, place on a lightly-greased baking tray, sprinkle with a touch of salt if you wish, and bake at 180°C/350°F/gas mark 4 for about 10 minutes. Serve the enchiladas with rice.

2 tablespoons olive oil	12 tortillas
1 small onion, chopped	350ml/12oz hot pepper sauce
225g/8oz chicken breast, cut	250ml/8fl oz no-salt-added
into 1cm/½ in squares	tomato sauce
275g/10oz cooked black beans	50g/2oz low-fat cheddar cheese,
100g/4oz green chillies,	grated
chopped	Low-fat yogurt
4 tablespoons chopped fresh	Chopped coriander
coriander or parsley	

Preheat oven to 180°C/350°F/gas mark 4.

In a large frying pan heat oil and sauté onion for 3 to 4 minutes or until softened. Add chicken, beans, and chillies, and simmer for 10 minutes or until chicken is cooked. Let mixture cool.

Heat tortillas gently. Spoon some filling along one edge and roll up the tortillas. Place each one, seam side down, in a large baking tin.

In a mixing bowl, combine hot pepper sauce and tomato sauce; pour over tortillas. Top with cheese and bake 25 to 30 minutes. Serve with yogurt and chopped coriander.

Indian Chickpea and Rice Biriyani

Makes 6 servings

Biriyani is the Indian word for this rice dish, which is another example of how another culture uses the combined amino acids from rice and beans to form a complete protein. While it can be a meal itself, you may prefer it as an accompaniment.

2 tablespoons corn oil
2 small onions, finely chopped
2 cloves garlic, crushed
1 red pepper, finely chopped
¼ teaspoon each ground
  cardamom, cayenne, cloves,
  coriander, ginger, and mace
½ teaspoon ground cinnamon
1 teaspoon ground cumin

200g/7oz long-grain rice
75g/3oz raisins
275g/10oz cooked or tinned
  chickpeas, drained and
  rinsed
3 tablespoons low-fat yogurt
Chopped coriander or parsley
  for garnish, optional

Preheat oven to 180°C/350°F/gas mark 4.

In a flameproof, ovenproof casserole heat oil and sauté onions and garlic, for 2 minutes. Add red pepper, cover, and simmer gently for 10 minutes, adding 3 tablespoons water or so, if you need to prevent burning.

Add spices, rice, raisins, chickpeas, and 450ml/¾ pint water. Bring liquid to a simmer, cover casserole, and place in the oven. Bake for 25 minutes. Remove cover, fluff up rice and chickpeas with a fork, and stir in yogurt. Garnish if you wish with chopped herbs and serve immediately.

Barley, Pepper, and Bean Curd Sauté

Makes 4 servings

Bean curd is another name for tofu, widely eaten around the world as a major source of protein. If you haven't eaten it before, try it this way to see how you like it as a meat alternative once in a while. If you don't like it at all, you can substitute chunks of turkey breast.

2 tablespoons olive oil
4 cloves garlic, crushed
2 red peppers, seeds and
    membranes removed, and
    thinly sliced
400g/14oz cooked pearl barley

2 tablespoons lemon or lime
    juice
225g/8oz bean curd, diced
225g/8oz fresh spinach,
    chopped
Pepper

In a large frying pan heat olive oil and sauté garlic for 30 seconds.
    Add peppers, cover, and simmer for 5 minutes over medium heat. Remove the cover and add barley and lemon juice.
    Stir for 5 minutes without a cover. Add bean curd and spinach. Cover and simmer over low heat for about another 5 minutes or until the spinach has wilted. Season to taste with pepper.

Tortilla and Black Bean Torte

Makes 4 servings

'Torte' usually refers to a dessert cake with many layers. This dish, however, is a multi-layered main course. I like it served with rice and a wedge of lemon. A glass of beer washes it down very nicely.

575g/20oz cooked black beans
2 tablespoons chopped red pepper
100g/4oz green chillies, chopped
1 teaspoon chilli or cumin powder

Tabasco to taste
2 tablespoons olive oil
8 tortillas
Low-fat yogurt, or chopped fresh tomatoes

Preheat oven to 180°C/350°F/gas mark 4.

In a blender or food processor, coarsely purée the black beans with the pepper, chillies, and chilli or cumin powder. Season to taste with Tabasco.

Heat olive oil in a large frying pan. When very hot, add the bean purée and sauté for 5 minutes, stirring constantly with a wooden spoon; remove from heat.

Place a tortilla on a baking sheet and spread with bean purée. Place another tortilla on top, press down, and layer with more purée. Continue until you have made a little 'torte' or cake of 4 tortillas with 3 layers of bean purée in between. Make another such torte. Cut each torte in 4 wedges and bake for 10 minutes or until hot throughout.

Serve with yogurt, or tomatoes to moisten the wedges, which might otherwise taste too dry.

MEAT AND POULTRY ENTRÉES

Pot Roast
Beef Stew and Wine
Chinese Stir-Fried Beef
Brazilian Black Bean and
  Beef Casserole
Savoury Pinto Beans and
  Beef
Meatloaf
Spectacular Meatloaf
Sloppy Joes
Hamburger and Meatball
  Preparation

Moroccan 'Tagine' (Stew) of
  Chickpeas and Beef
Pot au Feu
Spanish Lentil, Barley, and
  Ham Casserole
Black-Eyed Bean Casserole
  with Ham and Carrots
Hungarian Bean and
  Sauerkraut Stew with Ham
Cassoulet with Ham
Bean and Turkey Dinner
Jambalaya

All nutritional information listed in this section is based on 96 per cent fat-free ham or bacon. Please check food labels to ensure that this is the case with products you are purchasing.

Pot Roast

Makes 8 to 10 servings

This unique approach to preparing a beef roast is specially suited to a lean joint such as topside of beef.

2 tablespoons olive oil
4 small onions, thinly sliced
3 tablespoons red wine vinegar
2 teaspoons sugar
4 carrots, peeled and thinly
    sliced

4×250ml/8fl oz tins no-salt-
    added tomato sauce
1 teaspoon Worcestershire
    sauce
Pepper
1.5kg/3lb topside

Preheat oven to 180°C/350°F/gas mark 4.

Heat oil, in a large frying pan over medium heat and sauté onions for 4 to 5 minutes, stirring every now and then. Add vinegar and sugar and simmer 2 to 3 minutes. Add carrots, tomato sauce, and Worcestershire sauce. Simmer gently, covered, over low heat, for 30 minutes.

Place this sauce in the bottom of a roasting pan. Set roast on top of the sauce and cook for 1 hour, then turn oven off and let roast sit in oven for 1½ hours more. Remove roast from oven and slice or cut into cubes. Toss meat with sauce and serve.

Beef Stew with Wine

Makes 8 servings

My mother long ago taught me a trick to make very lean roasts juicier and more tender. About halfway through the cooking time, take out the meat and slice it. Then return the slices loosely to the juices for the balance of the time. The meat will not only be more tender but will absorb the flavours of the vegetables and seasonings. Serve with boiled or mashed potatoes.

2 tablespoons olive oil	**½ teaspoon thyme**
4 onions, thinly sliced	**1 bay leaf**
4 carrots, thinly sliced	**1kg/2lb joint of topside**
750ml/1 ¼ pints red wine	**Pepper**

In a medium-sized saucepan heat oil and sauté onions for 2 minutes. Cover and simmer for 10 minutes, adding water if the onions stick to the base.

Add carrots, red wine, thyme, bay leaf, and meat. Cover and simmer for 1½ hours or until the meat is somewhat tender. Remove bay leaf and discard.

Drain meat and vegetables through a colander, reserving the juices. Place juices in a small saucepan and reduce until only 250ml/8fl oz remains. Return meat, vegetables, and juices to the pan and simmer, covered, for 5 minutes or until heated through. Season to taste with pepper.

Chinese Stir-Fried Beef

Makes 4 servings

For a long while after I started to cut back seriously on saturated fat in my diet, I relied entirely on chicken and seafood to do my stir-fry cooking. Now I use a very lean beef and cook it very quickly, leaving it on the rare side for best flavour and juiciness.

450g/1lb fillet steak
2 tablespoons soya sauce
½ teaspoon powdered ginger
½ tablespoon sugar
½ tablespoon chilli paste
1 tablespoon sesame oil

1 tablespoon corn oil
1 small onion, finely chopped
1 garlic clove, crushed
225g/8oz tin sliced water
  chestnuts

Slice fillet steak, across the grain, into pieces about 2.5cm/1in square; set aside.

Combine soya sauce, ginger, sugar, and chilli paste in a small bowl and set aside for later.

In a large frying pan or wok heat sesame and corn oil. When oils are very hot and just about smoking, add onion and stir-fry for 1 minute. Add garlic, meat, and water chestnuts, and stir-fry for 2 minutes longer. Add soya-sauce mixture and sauté for 1 minute more. Serve immediately before meat toughens.

Brazilian Black Bean and Beef Casserole

Makes 8 servings

Orange zest gives this dish a distinctive flavour. Serve the casserole with
a salad and a mound of rice or barley.

3 tablespoons olive oil
1 stalk celery, finely chopped
2 carrots, finely chopped
2 onions, finely chopped
3 cloves garlic, crushed
*1 small red pepper, finely
  chopped*

½ teaspoon grated orange zest
*397g/14oz tin no-salt-added
  tomatoes*
*450g/1lb lean stewing beef, cut
  into 1cm/½ in cubes*
*575g/1 ¼ lb cooked black beans
  pepper*

In a large saucepan heat oil and add celery, carrots, onions, garlic
and red pepper. Cover and simmer gently for 5 minutes, stirring
every now and then to make sure vegetables are not sticking.

Add orange zest and tomatoes, along with meat. Cover and
simmer for 30 minutes, stirring every now and then. Add black
beans and simmer, uncovered, for 15 to 30 minutes more until
stew is nice and thick. Season to taste with pepper.

Savoury Pinto Beans and Beef

Makes 6 servings

The unusual taste and texture in this dish comes from the grated lean beef. The easiest way I've found to prepare the beef is to grate partially frozen steaks with a kitchen grater in the same way you'd grate carrots. Since the meat is in such small pieces, it takes just a flash in a very lightly greased nonstick pan to cook the meat through. Then add the beef to the rest of the ingredients just before serving.

225g/8oz dried pinto beans,
  soaked
1 tablespoon olive oil
1 small onion, finely chopped
1 clove garlic, crushed
100g/4oz green chillis, chopped

½ teaspoon cumin seeds
1 jalapeno pepper, deseeded
  and finely chopped
1 tomato, chopped
225g/8oz fillet of beef, grated

Place pinto beans and all other ingredients except beef in a medium-sized saucepan. Add enough water to cover the beans and bring to the boil. Reduce to a simmer and cook gently, covered, for 1½ hours or until beans are tender. Be sure to keep the beans covered with liquid at all times or some will not cook properly.

Meanwhile, heat a lightly greased nonstick frying pan until hot. Add beef and quickly stir-fry on all sides, about 30 seconds. Add to the beans when they are done, and serve at once.

Meatloaf

Makes 4 servings

Some meatloaf recipes call for a lot more ingredients and take a lot more time. This approach is straightforward and works nicely when you just don't have the time to do a lot of chopping. Serve it with potatoes mashed with skimmed milk and a side dish of vegetables.

450g/1lb lean minced beef   *3 tablespoons ketchup*
25g/1oz oat bran   *2 tablespoons chopped parsley*
1 egg white   *3 tablespoons skimmed milk*
2 teaspoons lemon juice   *Pepper*

Preheat oven to 180°C/350°F/gas mark 4. Lightly grease a 20×10cm/8×4in loaf tin and set aside.

Blend all of the above ingredients in a large mixing bowl and pat them into the prepared loaf tin. Cover loaf tin with foil, and bake for 45 minutes. Let meatloaf sit for 10 minutes before slicing and serving.

Spectacular Meatloaf

Makes 4 servings

Once upon a time, meatloaf was a meal you'd serve to your family but never to company. Here's a recipe, based on a high-fat version at a trendy Los Angeles restaurant, that you'll be proud to put on your table regardless of who's coming to dinner. It does take some time to prepare, but it's well worth the effort for special occasions. I like to serve this wonderful meatloaf with spinach and mashed potatoes.

100g/4oz each of spring onion
* and onion, grated*
50g/2oz each celery and carrot,
* grated*
25g/1oz each green and red
* pepper, grated*
2 garlic cloves, crushed
1 teaspoon salt and pepper
½ teaspoon each white pepper,
* ground cumin, ground*
* nutmeg*

¼ teaspoon cayenne pepper
100ml/4fl oz tomato ketchup
4 egg whites
100ml/4fl oz skimmed milk
450g/1lb each lean minced beef
* and turkey breast*
40g/1 ½ oz oat bran

Preheat the oven to 180°C/350°F/gas mark 4.

Lightly grease a large frying pan and sauté vegetables until soft and water has evaporated. Set aside to cool in large mixing bowl. Measure herbs and seasonings, blend together, and add to vegetables. Next add ketchup, egg whites, and milk, followed by meat, and finally the oat bran. Mix well and form into one or two loaves. Place in a baking tin, and bake for 50 to 55 minutes.

Spectacular meatloaf sauce

8 medium-sized shallots, grated
1 tablespoon ground thyme
3 bay leaves
½ teaspoon crushed black
* pepper*

450ml/ ¾ pt each dry white
* wine, chicken stock, beef*
* stock*

Lightly grease a frying pan and sauté shallots along with herbs and pepper until tender. Add wine and reduce to a glaze over high heat. Add beef and chicken stock and reduce over high heat until 450ml/¾ pint of sauce remains.

Spinach
Plan on 200g/7oz of spinach per person. Wash thoroughly to get rid of all the sand and grit. Pick off stems. Shake off water and place in large pot. Cover and cook with no added water over medium heat for 2 minutes. The little bit of moisture clinging to the spinach will cook it and it'll turn out emerald green and delicious.

Mashed potatoes
Plan on one medium-size potato per person. Place in cold water with optional salt. Bring to the boil uncovered, and simmer for 15 to 20 minutes until potatoes are tender to a fork. Drain and mash with enough skimmed milk to whip the potatoes as creamy as you like. Season with pepper and a pinch of grated nutmeg.

Sloppy Joes

Makes 4 servings

It may be years since your schoolroom days, but no one forgets childhood memories, and amongst mine are Sloppy Joes. Taste the mix before ladling it onto the hamburger rolls or muffins. The Sloppy Joes in my past might have been a bit sweeter than these, and I sometimes add a bit of granulated or brown sugar to taste.

1 tablespoon corn or olive oil	*450ml/¾ pint no-salt-added*
1 onion, finely chopped	*tomato sauce*
1 red pepper, finely chopped	*450g/1lb lean beef, minced*
2 teaspoons chilli powder	*4 hamburger rolls or muffins,*
½ teaspoon garlic powder	*split in half and toasted*

In a large frying pan heat oil and sauté onion and pepper for 5 minutes, stirring constantly. If vegetables begin to stick add a few tablespoons of water and cook until soft.

Add chilli powder, garlic, and tomato sauce and simmer 1 minute. Mash and stir meat into the sauce and simmer 2 minutes more, stirring constantly. What you are doing is getting rid of the red of the meat and heating it through; do not overcook.

Arrange 2 toasted rolls or muffin halves on each of 4 serving plates.

Spoon some of this mixture onto each of the bun halves and serve immediately.

Hamburger and Meatball Preparation

Makes 4 burgers

Simply season the meat with garlic and pepper, then form it into burgers, or add ingredients to make it a little more 'cholesterol-fighting'.

450g/1lb lean beef, minced	*½ teaspoon Worcestershire*
25g/1oz oat bran	*sauce*
1 egg white	*¼ teaspoon garlic powder*

To make and cook as hamburgers
Mix all of the above ingredients and shape into 4 burgers. Heat 1 tablespoon oil in a frying pan or use a nonstick pan. Sauté 3 minutes per side—not longer as this type of meat must be eaten rare or medium rare. Serve immediately.

To make and cook as meatballs
Mix all of the above ingredients and shape into 24 meatballs, each about 2.5cm/1in in size.

Bring 450ml/¾ pint no-salt-added tomato sauce to a simmer; add meatballs, cover, and simmer for 2 minutes. Turn meatballs over and cook, covered, for 2 minutes more. Do not overcook or meatballs will be dry; serve immediately as they are, or with spaghetti.

Moroccan 'Tagine' (Stew) of Chickpeas and Beef

Makes 4 servings

If you've never heard of 'tagine' don't feel too badly, I never did either until I met Michele Urvater, who came up with this recipe. Like all stews, this one needs to simmer quite a while to make the meat nice and tender.

2 tablespoons olive oil
1 medium onion, finely
  chopped
1 teaspoon ground ginger
1 teaspoon ground coriander
1 teaspoon ground cinnamon
2 apples, peeled, cored, and
  finely chopped

450g/1lb lean stewing beef
1 tablespoon honey
1 tablespoon tomato purée
200g/7oz stoned prunes
275g/10oz cooked or tinned
  chickpeas, drained and
  rinsed
Pepper

In a medium-sized saucepan heat olive oil and sauté onion for 2 minutes. Add spices and 100ml/4fl oz water, and simmer 5 minutes or until onions are soft. Stir in apples and meat, cover, and simmer gently for 1½ hours or until meat is tender.

Add honey, tomato purée, prunes, and chickpeas, and simmer for 30 minutes more. Season to taste with pepper. This stew tastes better and the texture of the meat becomes more tender if you make it a day in advance and reheat it for 45 minutes, at very low heat.

Pot au Feu

Makes 6 servings

This is basically a beef stew, made in the French manner. This version includes lean meat, along with white beans to add a cholesterol-lowering dimension.

3 carrots, peeled and cut into 1cm/½ in rounds
2 white turnips, peeled and cut into 2.5cm/1in pieces
225g/8oz raw white cabbage, shredded
2 onions, cut into 8 wedges
1 leek, washed and cut into 2.5cm/1in lengths
½ teaspoon dried thyme
397g/14oz tin no-salt-added tomatoes
225g/8oz very lean smoked ham, cut into 2.5cm/1in chunks

225g/8oz lean stewing beef cut into 1cm/½ in cubes
275g/10oz cooked or drained tinned haricot or white kidney beans
450g/1lb chicken breasts
Pepper
4 tablespoons chopped fresh herbs, such as dill or parsley, optional

In a large saucepan, place all ingredients, except beans, chicken, pepper and fresh herbs, and cover with 1.25 litres/2½ pints water. Slowly bring to the boil and, with a slotted spoon, remove any foam that rises to the top. Cover and simmer very gently for 1 hour, adding water to keep the level of the liquid constant.

Add beans and chicken and simmer for 10 minutes more. Season to taste with pepper and stir in dill or parsley if you wish.

Spanish Lentil, Barley, and Ham Casserole

Makes 6 to 8 servings

Casseroles mean easy preparation and easy clean-up. You can alter this recipe by replacing the ham with either chicken or fish. This casserole is cooked in the oven, but if you wish you can simmer it gently on top of the stove for about 1½ hours.

2 tablespoons olive oil
3 onions, finely chopped
2 carrots, finely chopped
1 stalk celery, finely chopped
1 clove garlic, crushed
2 tablespoons chopped red
* pepper*
225g/8oz very lean ham, cut
* into 1cm/½ in dice*

¼ teaspoon saffron
90g/3½ oz lentils
90g/3½ oz pearl barley
100ml/4fl oz dry white wine
450g/1lb potatoes, peeled and
* cut into 2.5cm/1in dice*
Pepper

Preheat oven to 180°C/350°F/gas mark 4.

In a very large flameproof casserole, heat olive oil over medium heat and stir in onions, carrots, celery, and garlic. Sauté for 2 to 3 minutes, stirring frequently. Add red pepper, ham, and saffron, and sauté for 1 minute. Add lentils, barley, and white wine, along with 750ml/1¼ pints water. Add potatoes and season to taste with pepper.

Bring liquid to a simmer, cover casserole, and place in oven. Cook for 45 minutes to an hour or until potatoes, lentils, and barley have absorbed all the liquid and are tender.

Black-Eyed Bean Casserole with Ham and Carrots

Makes 4 to 6 servings

With the beans, ham, and carrots, this dish is truly a meal in a pot. In my house we have a wonderful alternative to the ham—sausages specially made with turkey breast, with virtually no fat at all. If you know a butcher who makes his own sausages, ask him to prepare some for you with turkey breast, using all the usual herbs and spices.

575g/1 ¼ lb cooked black-eyed
  beans
1 teaspoon dried sage
250ml/8fl oz no-salt-added
  tomato sauce
½ teaspoon garlic powder

4 carrots, peeled and grated
225g/8oz lean smoked ham,
  diced
2 tablespoons olive oil
Pepper

Preheat oven to 180°C/350°F/gas mark 4.

Combine all ingredients in a mixing bowl, then transfer to a 25 × 33cm/9 × 13in ovenproof dish. Cover and bake for 30 minutes.

Hungarian Bean and Sauerkraut Stew with Ham

Makes 8 servings

Paprika gives Hungarian stews their distinctive flavour. The recipe calls for ham, but you can also use salmon in this dish. If you choose to do so, add the fish during the last 10 minutes of simmering.

2 tablespoons olive oil
2 onions, finely chopped
2 tablespoons paprika
1 tablespoon caraway seeds
1kg/2lb sauerkraut, drained
450g/1lb very lean ham, cut
   into 1cm/½ in cubes

575g/1 ¼ lb cooked or drained
   and rinsed tinned haricot or
   white kidney beans
2 tablespoons finely chopped
   fresh dill or 2 teaspoons
   dried dill
Pepper

In a large saucepan heat oil. When very hot, add onions, cover, and simmer gently for 5 minutes, stirring every now and then to make sure onions are not sticking.

Remove pan from heat and stir paprika and caraway into the onions. Return pot to the heat and add sauerkraut, ham, and beans. Cover and simmer for 30 minutes, stirring every now and then. Stir in dill and season to taste with pepper.

Cassoulet with Ham

Makes 8 servings

Traditional cassoulet is laden with fat from goose, duck, and lamb. We can preserve all the flavour with practically none of the fat by long simmering of the soaked dried beans and by using ham.

4 tablespoons olive oil
4 cloves garlic, crushed
1 large onion, finely chopped
2 carrots, finely chopped
397/14oz tin no-salt-added
tomatoes
1 teaspoon thyme

225g/8oz very lean smoked
ham, cut into 1cm/½ in dice
Pepper
450g/1lb haricot beans, soaked
and drained
50g/2oz seasoned oat-bran
crumbs (see page 236)

Preheat oven to 180°C/350°F/gas mark 4.

In a flameproof casserole, heat olive oil and sauté garlic, onion, and carrots, for 3 to 4 minutes. Add tomatoes, thyme, and ham, and sauté for a minute more; season to taste with pepper. Stir in beans and add just enough water to cover. Bring liquid to the boil, reduce to a simmer, cover, and place in oven.

Bake for 1½ hours. Uncover casserole, sprinkle with crumbs, and bake for 30 minutes to an hour more or until beans have absorbed liquid and top is somewhat crusty.

Bean and Turkey Dinner

Makes 6 servings

Instead of the usual meat sauce with your next meal of spaghetti, try this
dish as an alternative.

2 tablespoons olive or corn oil
1 onion, finely chopped
4 carrots, finely chopped
450g/1lb minced turkey breast
100ml/4fl oz no-salt-added
  tomato sauce
½ teaspoon oregano

275g/10oz freshly cooked or
  drained and rinsed tinned
  beans, such as red kidney
  beans, haricot beans, or
  chickpeas
Pepper
4 tablespoons chopped parsley

In a large frying pan heat olive oil, add onion and carrots and stir-
fry for 5 minutes. Add turkey and stir-fry, breaking up turkey,
until there is no more pink. Add tomato sauce, oregano, and
beans, and season to taste with pepper. Stir-fry for another minute
or so, or until all ingredients are very hot. Stir in parsley and serve
immediately.

Jambalaya

Makes 8 servings

Louisiana cuisine didn't get famous for nothing. But one of its star dishes, jambalaya, almost always comes loaded with fat in the form of sausage. This recipe substitutes chicken breast, losing the fat and keeping all the flavour. Make it as hot and spicy as you like. Good jambalaya is meant to be a bit soupy; don't be ashamed to mop it up with a chunk of bread.

2 tablespoons olive oil
2 onions, finely chopped
2 red peppers, finely chopped
4 stalks celery, finely chopped
2 teaspoons dried thyme
½ teaspoon sage
½ -1 teaspoon cayenne pepper
1 bay leaf
900ml/1 ½ pints no-salt-added tomato sauce

675g/1 ½ lb skinless, boneless chicken breasts, cut into 1cm/½ in cubes
400g/14oz parboiled long-grain rice
25g/1oz rice bran
2 spring onions, thinly sliced, optional

In a very large saucepan, heat olive oil, stir in onions, peppers, and celery, and stir-fry for a minute or so. Add a few tablespoons of water, cover, and simmer gently, stirring on occasion, for 8 to 10 minutes or until vegetables are soft.

Add thyme, sage, cayenne, bay leaf, and tomato sauce and simmer for 2 minutes. Add chicken, rice, and rice bran, along with 900ml/1½ pints water. Bring liquid to a simmer, stir, cover, and cook gently for 20 minutes, or until rice is tender.

Remove pan from heat, stir ingredients together, cover and leave, off heat, for 10 minutes. Remove bay leaf, turn into a serving dish, garnish with spring onions if you wish, and serve.

VARIATION. You can turn this into a vegetarian main course by substituting 450g/1lb cooked or tinned red kidney beans for the diced chicken.

FISH ENTRÉES

Poached Salmon Steaks
Poached Salmon with Green
  Sauce
Teriyaki Salmon
Blackened Cajun Salmon
Salmon Bouillabaisse
Salmon Kebabs
Salmon Barley Pilaff
Salmon and Vegetable
  Packages
Warm 'Seviche' of Salmon

Fish and Fibre Stew
Scandinavian Salmon-Rice
  Stew
Soused Mackerel
Baked Sardines and
  Chickpeas
Sardine and Potato Pie
Mackerel Parmigiana
Grilled Mackerel with Spicy
  Dressing
Fish Paella

Poached Salmon Steaks

Makes 6 servings

Many people enjoy a fine luncheon of chilled salmon when eating out in restaurants but don't think of preparing the dish at home. Yet poaching is one of the easiest and most foolproof methods of cooking fish. This recipe can be prepared well in advance. Serve it with a crisp green salad and bread.

6×175g/6oz salmon **steaks, fresh or frozen**
100ml/4fl oz **dry white wine**
½ **teaspoon dill seed**

DRESSING (or use *450ml/¾ pint* Chickpea Russian Dressing, Page 132)
4 **tablespoons reduced-calorie mayonnaise**
75g/3oz **diced tofu**
3 **tablespoons white wine vinegar**
3 **tablespoons finely chopped fresh dill**

Place salmon steaks in a single layer in a large stainless steel saucepan. Cover with white wine and dill seed. Add enough water to just cover the salmon steaks. Slowly bring liquid to a simmer and simmer 2 minutes. Remove salmon from heat and let the steaks cool to room temperature in this cooking liquid; this will keep them moist. When cool, remove salmon from the cooking liquid and place on a platter; chill, covered for 1 hour.

Meanwhile, in a blender or food processor, combine mayonnaise, tofu, vinegar, and dill, and blend until smooth; if the dressing is too thick, thin with water to the desired consistency. Serve with chilled salmon.

Poached Salmon with Green Sauce

Makes 2 servings

For poaching, you can use plain water, a combination of water and some dry white wine, or, better still, a court bouillon such as the one I've described here. Most preparations can be done ahead so you can just pop the salmon into the court bouillon and to your guests it'll look as though you're one of those people who can entertain effortlessly. This recipe is for just two people, for a nice candlelit dinner, but you can double or triple the amounts if you wish.

COURT BOUILLON
1.15 litres/2 pints water
Juice of ½ lemon
2 small carrots, thinly sliced
1 small onion, sliced

2 bay leaves
6 peppercorns
1 teaspoon salt, optional
2 salmon steaks, 2.5cm/1in thick

GREEN SAUCE
3 tablespoons plain low-fat
  yogurt
1½ tablespoons reduced-
  calorie mayonnaise
¼ teaspoon salt, optional

½ teaspoon white vinegar
1 spring onion, finely chopped
5 tablespoons chopped fresh
  dill or 2 tablespoons dried
Parsley and lemon for garnish

Preheat oven to 180°C/350°F/gas mark 4. Place all court bouillon ingredients in a shallow flameproof casserole and bring up to the boil, then simmer for 10 minutes. Slice remaining lemon half into thin circular slices (you may do this in advance). Place salmon in casserole, spoon ingredients over the salmon pieces and top with sliced lemon. Cover with a piece of greaseproof paper and bake for 20 minutes.

You can prepare the green sauce in advance or while salmon is poaching in the oven. Simply place all ingredients in a blender and blend at high speed until well mixed, stopping the blender occasionally to scrape down the sides. By the way, using fresh dill makes all the difference in the world. The recipe yields 4 servings of sauce.

Teriyaki Salmon

Of all the fish that swim the seas, my all-around favourite remains salmon. How happy I was to discover it's one of the richest fish in omega-3 fish oils. You can substitute mackerel or other fish in this or any of my recipes with no problem. This is a truly simple yet delicious meal that you can serve to friends with pride. Just marinate the fish for a while before you grill it.

MARINADE
150ml/¼ pint low-salt soya
  sauce
3 tablespoons sweet sherry
1 tablespoon brown sugar
½ teaspoon freshly grated
  ginger root

1 large garlic clove, crushed
Juice of 1 lemon
450g/1lb salmon **steaks or fillets**

Mix together marinade ingredients in a large plastic storage bag, place fish in the bag and cover with the marinade. Marinate in the fridge for 2 to 3 hours. Drain and grill for 3 minutes on each side.

Serve with mounds of steamed rice and a pile of stir-fried bamboo shoots and bean sprouts.

Blackened Cajun Salmon

When Chef Paul Prudhomme hit the scene with his Cajun cooking in New Orleans, he caused an actual shortage of various kinds of red fish, which he specialized in blackening. As he later pointed out, blackening works well with many fish and I think one of the best for this approach is salmon. You can make your own blackening seasoning to keep on hand for this and other dishes as well. There's only one drawback to making blackened fish: expect an enormous amount of smoke when the margarine and fish hit the searing-hot cast-iron frying pan. I deal with this by putting the frying pan directly on charcoal on the barbecue grill outside. It's just too smoky to cook indoors.

8 tablespoons paprika	*4 tablespoons oregano*
5 tablespoons garlic powder	*2 tablespoons dried basil*
4 tablespoons cayenne	*2 tablespoons onion powder*
4 tablespoons black pepper	*1 tablespoon salt (optional)*
4 tablespoons ground thyme	

Mix all seasonings together and store in a tightly closed container. Sprinkle seasonings liberally over salmon fillets (you can use steaks, but the fillets work a lot better). Place seasoned salmon along with a small pat of margarine in a *very* hot cast-iron frying pan. Sear for 2 minutes, then turn, using another pat of margarine to blacken the other side for another 2 minutes. This is a spicy dish, and a glass of cold beer fits the bill perfectly.

Salmon Bouillabaisse

Makes 4 hearty servings

I just love bouillabaisse, and find that every restaurant's version is a bit different. One thing I've never seen, though, in this marvellously aromatic soup, is salmon. So here's the way I make it at home. I've also included a classic recipe for rouille, which is a condiment you add to the bouillabaisse just before serving or at the table. It is optional but adds a nice touch. Serve this meal with some crusty French bread and a bottle of red wine.

450g/1lb salmon steaks or fillets cut into pieces
225g/8oz shrimp, lobster, crab, or a combination of all
8 clams or mussels
1 tablespoon olive oil
2 leeks (chopped white portion only)
1 medium onion, chopped

2 garlic cloves, chopped
1 large tomato cut into wedges
Water or fish stock to cover
Bouquet garni (thyme, bay leaf, parsley, celery, rosemary)
Pinch of saffron
Salt, pepper, and cayenne to taste

Heat olive oil in a large saucepan and add vegetables, sautéing them until onion becomes transparent. Add water or fish stock along with the bouquet garni and simmer for 5 minutes. Add salmon and shrimp and simmer for 5 more minutes. Add clams or mussels and simmer for a final 5 minutes, or until the shells open.

Add a healthy pinch of saffron, and season with salt, pepper, and cayenne to taste. That's all there is to it! You never want to prepare this dish in advance; it should be served immediately, so the fish and vegetables remain firm, not mushy. You may add the rouille as you serve the bouillabaisse, or each person can add it to his or her own bowl.

Rouille

2 *garlic cloves*
1 *small red pepper*
1 *tablespoon* oat bran or apple
   fibre

2 *tablespoons stock*
1 *tablespoon olive oil*
½ *teaspoon paprika*
1 *tablespoon tomato purée*

Put all ingredients into a blender or food processor and blend until smooth.

Salmon Kebabs

Makes 4 servings

There's something really festive about skewering foods to barbecue or grill. This recipe provides a particularly colourful dish. Serve it with lots of steamed rice and a nice bottle of crisp white wine.

Juice of 1 large lemon
Juice of 1 lime
3 tablespoons olive oil
1 small onion, finely chopped
1 clove garlic, crushed
1 teaspoon crushed red pepper
   flakes
1 teaspoon rosemary

450g/1lb salmon *steaks, cut*
   into chunks
1 green pepper, cut into
   5cm/2in pieces
1 red pepper, cut into 5cm/2in
   pieces
8 large mushrooms

Mix juice, oil, onion, garlic, pepper flakes, and rosemary in a large plastic storage bag. Add pieces of salmon, peppers, and mushrooms. Marinate in fridge for 2 hours. Skewer salmon, peppers, and mushrooms alternately and barbecue or grill 3 minutes per side. Do not overcook; serve immediately.

Salmon Barley Pilaff

Makes 6 servings

Barley brings additional soluble fibre to this pilaff. Salmon delivers its
protective oils. And vinegar gives the dish piquancy. While the recipe
calls for either rice or white wine vinegar, you might want to experiment
with other vinegars as well.

1 tablespoon olive oil
1 onion, finely chopped
1 carrot, finely chopped
1 celery stalk, finely chopped
2 × 200g/7oz tins salmon,
*   drained*

200g/7oz pearl barley
3 tablespoons white wine or
*   rice vinegar*
3 tablespoons finely chopped
*   parsley or coriander*
Pepper

Preheat oven to 180°C/350°F/gas mark 4.

In a large flameproof casserole heat olive oil and sauté onion,
carrot, and celery for 2 to 3 minutes, stirring constantly.

Add salmon and stir around to break up the fish, then stir in
barley, vinegar, herb and 450ml/¾ pint water. Season to taste
with pepper. Bring liquid to a simmer, cover, and cook in the oven
for 45 minutes or until barley has absorbed all the liquid and is
just tender to the bite. Stir ingredients around with a fork just
before serving.

Salmon and Vegetable Packages

Makes 6 servings

Where do I begin listing the advantages of this cooking approach? First, I guess, would be that the recipe is absolutely foolproof; it just can't fail. Second, it takes little preparation time. Third, you can make up the packages ahead of time in case you're on a tight schedule after work or when entertaining. Fourth, you have no pots and pans to clean, just toss out the foil. Fifth, and probably the most important, the dish is delish!

6×175g/6oz salmon **steaks**
4 celery stalks
1 parsnip, peeled
2 carrots, peeled (or 4 carrots if you don't have the parsnip)

6 tablespoons white wine
2 teaspoons sugar
Pepper

Preheat oven to 190°C/375°F/gas mark 5.

Place each salmon steak on a piece of lightly greased aluminium foil, about 25cm/10in square and set aside.

Cut celery, parsnip, and carrots into thin strips, about 5cm/2in long and 5mm/¼in thick. Simmer these in the white wine and sugar, in a covered frying pan over medium heat, for about 10 to 15 minutes or until tender.

Spoon some of this vegetable mixture on top of each salmon steak, and season to taste with pepper. Bring all four corners of each piece of foil to the centre; crimp them together to enclose the fish. Set the packages on a baking tray and bake for 30 minutes.

Open packages and serve salmon with the vegetables and natural juices.

Warm 'Seviche' of Salmon

Makes 6 servings

Here's a dish with two compromises. First, seviche is normally made with scallops; we've substituted salmon. Second, seviche is 'cooked' during the marinade process; here we cook the salmon in the oven after marinating, and serve it warm, along with the marinating mixture and pan juices. If fresh coriander is unavailable, substitute another fresh herb such as parsley, although the flavour will be less than authentic. I serve this with baked cherry tomatoes with herbs sprinkled on top.

6×175g/6oz fresh salmon steaks
½ onion, finely chopped
1 clove garlic, crushed
6 tablespoons finely chopped
*   coriander leaves*

3 tablespoons each lemon and
*   lime juice*
1 tablespoon olive oil
Cayenne pepper to taste

Set salmon steaks in an ovenproof enamel or glass dish. Mix onion, garlic, coriander, lemon and lime juices, and olive oil. Season to taste with cayenne and pour over the salmon steaks. Cover dish and refrigerate for 6 hours at least or, preferably, overnight.

Preheat oven to 180°C/350°F/gas mark 4. Place the covered dish of salmon in the oven, and bake for 15 to 20 minutes or until just cooked through. Serve with the juices.

Fish and Fibre Stew

Makes 8 servings

Here's the ultimate healthy stew. You get the protective oils of the salmon in the same dish with soluble fibre from the lentils and peas. At the same time we balance the meal with vegetables. If you wish, you can even add some chunks of potato when you cook the vegetables. Serve with some crusty bread and you have all four food groups represented.

90g/3 ½ oz dried lentils
90g/3 ½ oz dried split green peas
397g/14oz tin no-salt-added tomatoes
1 small onion, finely chopped
1 small red pepper, finely chopped

1 carrot, finely chopped
1 stalk celery, finely chopped
450g/1lb salmon, cut into chunks
450g/1lb tin cannellini beans
275g/10oz sweetcorn kernels
Pepper

In a large saucepan bring to the boil lentils, split peas, tomatoes, onions, peppers, carrot, celery, and 450ml/¾ pint water. Simmer, covered, for 25 minutes.

Add salmon, beans, liquid from the tin, and the sweetcorn. If needed, add some water to just cover mixture. Cover and simmer for 15 minutes more or until lentils and peas are cooked through and tender; season to taste with pepper and serve.

Scandinavian Salmon-Rice Stew

Makes 6 servings

There's no question about it, salmon is my favourite dish. One of the reasons is its versatility, which this Scandinavian dish demonstrates beautifully.

250ml/8fl oz Clamato juice
6 tablespoons white wine
3 tablespoons finely chopped parsnip
1 small carrot, finely chopped
1 onion, finely chopped
40g/1½ oz long-grain white rice

275g/10oz frozen spinach, thawed
3 tablespoons rice bran
2×200g/7oz tins salmon, drained
3 tablespoons finely chopped fresh dill or parsley

In a large saucepan bring to the boil Clamato, white wine, 450ml/¾ pint water, parsnips, carrots, onion, rice, and spinach. Simmer, covered, for 10 minutes.

Add rice bran, salmon, and dill, and simmer 5 minutes more.

Soused Mackerel

Makes 6 servings

Mackerel is very rich in omega-3 fish oils, and mackerel lovers will enjoy this dish served hot with potatoes or rice, or chilled with salad. Those who aren't so fond of mackerel might want to substitute tinned salmon.

675g/1 ½ lb mackerel *fillets*
250ml/8fl oz no-salt-added
   tomato sauce
225g/8oz cocktail onions
2 tablespoons rice or white
   wine vinegar

1 teaspoon prepared mustard
Pinch ground nutmeg and/or
   mace

Preheat oven to 180°C/350°F/gas mark 4.

Dice the mackerel and place in a 23cm/9in square ovenproof dish.

In a small bowl, mix the tomato sauce with the cocktail onions, vinegar, mustard, and spices. Pour over fish and mix. Cook for 30 minutes. Serve hot or cool to room temperature and chill overnight before serving.

Baked Sardines and Chickpeas

Makes 6 servings

Here's your chance to get the benefits of both soluble fibre and fish oil in one dish. As always, you can substitute tinned salmon for the sardines. This is great served with rice.

2×450g/16oz tins chickpeas,
   drained and rinsed
3×120g/4oz tins sardines,
   drained and patted dry
250ml/8fl oz no-salt-added
   tomato sauce

1 teaspoon garlic powder
1 tablespoon dried parsley
Pepper
2 tablespoons Parmesan cheese

Preheat oven to 180°C/350°F/gas mark 4.

Mix all ingredients in a 23 × 33cm/9in × 13in ovenproof dish and bake for 20 to 25 minutes.

Sardine and Potato Pie

Makes 6 servings

This was inspired by shepherds pie. You can adapt the idea of using mashed potatoes as a topping for the pie to other recipes that normally use a traditional pie crust. In this dish you can substitute tinned salmon for the sardines if you prefer.

675g/1 ½ lb potatoes
3 tablespoons skimmed milk
Pepper
6 tablespoons chopped fresh
  parsley or dill
2 tablespoons olive oil

1 onion, thinly sliced
3 small red or green peppers,
  thinly sliced
Red pepper flakes, optional
3 × 120g/4oz tins sardines,
  drained

Peel potatoes and cut into 2.5cm/1in cubes. Boil in water to cover for about 20 to 25 minutes, or until tender. Drain, and mash with the milk. Do not mash them in the food processor or they will become gummy. Season to taste with pepper and blend in parsley or dill.

Preheat oven to 180°C/350°F/gas mark 4.

In a large frying pan, heat olive oil. When hot, add onion and peppers, and sauté, stirring constantly, for 3 to 4 minutes. Add 100ml/4fl oz of water, cover, and simmer for 10 minutes more, or until tender. Remove cover and cook, over medium-high heat, for about 5 minutes, or until all the liquid has evaporated. Season to taste with red pepper flakes if you wish. Stir in sardines and break them up a bit.

Scoop onion, pepper, and sardines into a 25cm/10in ovenproof pie plate. Pat mashed potatoes on top and bake for 30 minutes.

Mackerel Parmigiana

Makes 4 servings

Here, too, you can substitute salmon or any other fish for the mackerel.
The oatmeal gives the fish a lovely crunchy coating. I like this served with
pasta and a small salad.

450ml/¾ pint no-salt-added
  tomato sauce, seasoned with
  ½ teaspoon oregano
675g/1 ½ lb mackerel *fillets*
25g/½ oz oat bran

1 egg white mixed with 2
  tablespoons water
100g/4oz oatmeal
1 tablespoon corn oil
3 tablespoons Parmesan cheese

Preheat oven to 180°C/350°F/gas mark 4.

Pour seasoned tomato sauce into an ovenproof dish and set
aside.

Cut fillets into 4 portions. Dip fillets first into oat bran, then
into egg-white mixture, and then pat on the oatmeal to cover all
sides.

Heat oil in a large frying pan, over high heat. When very hot,
add fish, skin side facing up, and sauté for 1½ minutes. With a
spatula, turn fish over and sauté for a minute more. Transfer fish
to the ovenproof dish skin side down. Bake for 10 to 15 minutes,
depending on thickness. Sprinkle cheese over fish and sauce and
bake 5 minutes more.

Grilled Mackerel with Spicy Dressing

Makes 4 servings

The dressing gives a spicy and crunchy contrast to the rich flesh of the fish. For added colour try using both red and green peppers. And if mackerel isn't available, salmon can be substituted.

675g/1 ½ lb mackerel *fillets*
4 teaspoons olive oil + 2
  tablespoons
2 tablespoons wine vinegar
6 tablespoons finely chopped
  fresh parsley

1 red or green pepper, seeds
  and membranes removed,
  finely chopped
2 spring onions, thinly sliced
Pepper

Preheat grill.

Set fillets on grill pan and lightly brush their tops with olive oil. Grill for 10 to 15 minutes, depending on their thickness; take care not to overcook.

While fish is grilling, in a mixer or blender combine the 2 tablespoons oil, vinegar, parsley, green pepper, and spring onions; season to taste with pepper.

When fish is cooked through, spoon a quarter of the dressing over each fillet and serve immediately.

Fish Paella

Makes 6 to 8 servings

Many restaurants stake their claim to fame on their paella recipes. This dish is loved from coast to coast and around the world. Here's a variation on the theme, with salmon or mackerel substituted for the usual chicken, and rice bran supplying the creamy texture. Try it with a glass of Spanish wine, if you like.

2 tablespoons olive oil
1 onion, finely chopped
1 clove garlic, crushed
2 red or green peppers, finely
  chopped
100ml/4fl oz white wine
275g/10oz long-grain rice
⅛ - ¼ teaspoon saffron threads
250ml/8fl oz no-salt-added
  tomato sauce

25g/1oz finely ground rice bran
275g/10oz frozen petit pois,
  thawed
675g/1 ½ lb salmon or mackerel
  fillets, cut into 2.5cm/1in
  cubes
Pepper

In a large frying pan or saucepan heat olive oil and sauté the onion, garlic, and red or green peppers for 3 minutes, stirring continuously. Add white wine and simmer for 3 minutes more.

Stir in rice, saffron, and tomato sauce, along with 450ml/¾ pint water. Bring to a boil and simmer, covered, for 15 minutes.

Stir in rice bran, peas, and fish, and season to taste with pepper. Cover and simmer for 5 minutes more or until fish is just cooked through and rice is just tender to the bite.

SIDE DISHES

Beans and Legumes
Refried Beans
Bean Pancakes
Easy Baked Beans
Spiced Baked Beans
Bean and Artichoke Casserole
Pinto Bean Succotash
Purée of Butter Beans and
    Carrots
Broad Bean and Garlic Purée
Scandinavian White Bean
    and Rice Stew
Baked Chickpea Casserole
Chickpea, Garlic, and Thyme
    Purée
Black Bean Cakes
Black Beans and Rice Medley
Creole Red Beans and Rice
Braised Red Kidney Beans
    and Cabbage
Red Bean Stir-Fry
Red Beans with Garlic and
    Ginger
Barbecued Kidney Beans
Split Pea and Potato Purée
Pease Pudding

French Bean Casserole
Mixed Beans and Squash
Mixed Vegetable and Bean
    Pudding
Persian Rice and Lentils
Sweet Swedish Lentils
Sweet-and-Sour Lentils

**Rice Bran and Oat Bran
Dishes**
Artichoke and Chicken
    Risotto
Mushroom Risotto
Risotto Milanese
Indian Rice Pilaff
Rice and Carrot Pancakes
Chilled Tomato and Vegetable
    Purée
Spring Onion, and Oat-Bran
    Johnnycakes
Carrot and Potato Pancakes

Barley
Barley and Green Pea Medley
Chinese Fried Barley
Mushroom Barley Pilaff

Refried Beans

Makes 4 to 6 servings

An absolute must when enjoying Mexican food, refried beans traditionally are made with lard. This basic recipe calls for healthy olive oil instead. You can further enhance the recipe by adding one or more of the following: two large garlic cloves, crushed; a dash or two of Tabasco; one teaspoon salt (if your sodium limitations permit). If you add the garlic, sauté it along with the onion.

2 tablespoons olive oil	**Lime juice, optional**
1 small onion, finely chopped	**Chopped fresh coriander,**
2×450g/1lb tins red kidney	**optional**
beans	

In a large frying pan, heat oil. When hot, add onion and sauté for 2 to 3 minutes. Drain one of the tins of beans.

Add to the frying pan one tin of beans with liquid and the drained beans. Turn heat up fairly high and begin to mash the beans, with the edge of a wooden spoon, until they are coarsely broken down.

Reduce heat to low and simmer gently, stirring continuously with a wooden spoon, for 5 to 10 minutes, or until the beans form a coarse purée, which begins to stick to the bottom of the pan.

Serve as it is or lightly seasoned with drops of lime juice and coriander.

Bean Pancakes

Makes 12 pancakes

You can use this recipe as a blueprint for any dried-bean pancakes. They make an interesting appetizer or can be served with an apple sauce as a side dish with dinner.

275g/10oz cooked or drained tinned chickpeas or other beans, lentils, or split peas
2 spring onions, chopped
4 tablespoons chopped red pepper

6 tablespoons flour
1 teaspoon cumin seeds or other spice of your choice
2 egg whites
Corn oil

Preheat oven to 120°C/250°F/gas mark ½.

In a blender or food processor, combine chickpeas, spring onions, red pepper, flour, and cumin. Add about 4 tablespoons water to make a somewhat loose dough.

Beat egg whites until stiff and fold into batter.

Heat a large frying pan, preferably nonstick. Brush surface lightly with oil. Drop 3 tablespoons of batter for each pancake onto frying pan. With the back of a spoon, gently spread the pancake until it is quite thin. Cook for 3 to 4 minutes each side.

Keep cooked pancakes warm in oven, while you make more.

Easy Baked Beans

Makes about 6 servings

Baked beans come in many forms, from the Boston baked beans served in a ceramic pot to the kind heated over a camp fire. The kind you buy tinned in the supermarket are almost always made with saturated fat and are lacking in flavour. This recipe gives you all the flavour with none of the saturated fat. It calls for one of three kinds of beans, but you might also try using all three types in the same dish.

3 tablespoons brown sugar
2 tablespoons molasses
3 tablespoons Dijon mustard
4 tablespoons ketchup
1 teaspoon garlic powder

Pepper
3 × 450g/1lb tins haricot,
    cannellini, or white kidney
    beans

Preheat oven to 180°C/350°F/gas mark 4.

In a bowl combine brown sugar, molasses, mustard, ketchup and garlic, and season to taste with pepper. Stir in beans and transfer to a baking dish. Cover and bake for 30 minutes; uncover and bake for 15 minutes more.

Spiced Baked Beans

Makes 8 servings

Someday when the weather is cold and the wind roaring, you might like to try an old-fashioned cook-all-day baked-bean recipe. This is the way grandmother cooked, and it fills the house with the aromas that memories are made of.

450g/1lb haricot, chickpeas, or small white beans, soaked (see page 80) and drained
450ml/¾ pint fat-free chicken stock or water
1 medium onion, finely chopped
100g/4oz very lean ham, chopped

4 cloves garlic, crushed
½ teaspoon ground cumin
¼ teaspoon ground cloves
¼ teaspoon mace
Pepper
3 tablespoons molasses

Preheat oven to 150°C/350°F/gas mark 2.

In a very large flameproof casserole, combine all ingredients and stir until mixed. Add 900ml/1½ pints of water, bring to a simmer on top of the cooker, cover, and bake for 6 hours.

Increase the oven heat to 180°C/350°F/gas mark 4. Uncover the casserole and bake for 45 minutes to an hour more, or until the beans have absorbed all the liquid and formed a slight crust on top.

Bean and Artichoke Casserole

Makes 4 to 6 servings

Served with rice this can make a very attractive vegetarian meal. If you prefer serve it as a side dish with a piece of grilled lean steak.

2 × 450g/1lb borlotti or pinto
  beans
450g/1lb tin artichoke hearts,
  drained and chopped

Small pinch each of cayenne
  and ground cloves
½ teaspoon ground cumin
2 tablespoons chilli sauce

Preheat oven to 180°C/350°F/gas mark 4.

Empty one tin of beans and liquid into a 23cm/9in square ovenproof dish. Drain and rinse the other tin of beans, then roughly chop the beans. Add chopped beans and artichokes to the whole beans. Add spices and chilli sauce and mix together well.

Place dish in oven, uncovered, and bake for 30 minutes.

Pinto Bean Succotash

Makes 4 to 6 servings

The Indians introduced colonial American settlers to succotash, a medley of sweetcorn and butter beans. This version also delivers soluble fibre by way of the apple fibre, which thickens the sauce and adds a touch of sweetness. Try it with lean gammon steaks.

4 tablespoons apple fibre
100ml/4fl oz skimmed milk
2 tablespoons ketchup
Pepper

275g/10oz cooked pinto beans
**200g/7oz thawed sweetcorn
  kernels**
Small jar cocktail onions

In a medium-sized saucepan, bring apple fibre, milk, 3 tablespoons water, and ketchup to a slow boil, stirring all the time, preferably with a whisk. Season to taste with pepper.

Stir in beans, sweetcorn, and onions, and simmer, uncovered, for 15 minutes or until the flavours come together and the sauce thickens a bit more.

Purée of Butter Beans and Carrots

Makes 4 to 6 servings

This is an interesting and delicious side dish, with a creamy texture that goes well with turkey or ham.

1 tablespoon vegetable oil
150g/2oz carrot, finely
   chopped
1 small onion, finely chopped
150g/5oz dried butter beans,
   soaked (see page 80) and
   drained

200ml/7fl oz skimmed milk
¼ teaspoon ground nutmeg
Pepper

In a medium-sized saucepan, heat oil and sauté carrot and onion for 1 minute, stirring frequently. Add beans, 450ml/¾ pint water, half the milk, and nutmeg. Bring to a simmer, reduce heat to very low, and cook, partially covered, for 45 to 50 minutes or until the beans are tender. If the mixture looks a little curdled, don't worry; this all works itself out in the mashing or puréeing.

While beans are cooking, stir them occasionally to prevent them from sticking; if the liquid is evaporating too quickly, add the extra milk. When cooked, mash the beans with a wooden spoon or, if you prefer a smooth texture, purée in a blender or food processor. Season well with pepper.

Broad Bean and Garlic Purée

Makes 4 to 6 servings

Wine, garlic, and thyme complement the flavour of the broad bean nicely. You must use a drinking-quality wine rather than a cooking wine in this dish, or the flavour will become harsh and unpleasant.

2×450g/1lb tins broad
   beans
4 cloves garlic, crushed
1 teaspoon dried thyme

*450ml/¾ pint drinking-
   quality dry red wine, such
   as Burgundy*
Pepper

Gently simmer the beans and their liquid, garlic, thyme, red wine, and 450ml/¾ pint water, partially covered, for 45 minutes or until the beans have absorbed all the liquid.

Mash the beans against the sides of the pan until you form a purée. If you do not like the texture of their skins, pass the beans through a food processor to make a smoother purée. Season to taste with pepper.

Scandinavian White Bean and Rice Stew

Makes 8 servings

Combining beans and rice yields high-quality protein. Combining two, three, or four kinds of beans provides interesting taste and texture. And fresh herbs give this dish wonderful flavour; by all means try to use fresh dill rather than dried whenever possible.

200g/7oz long-grain rice
275g/10oz cooked or drained
  and rinsed tinned haricot, or
  white kidney beans
2 tablespoons lemon juice

4 tablespoons chopped fresh
  dill or 1 tablespoons dried
  dill weed
Pepper

Place rice, beans, lemon juice, and 450ml/¾ pint water in a large saucepan and bring to the boil. Cover and simmer for 20 minutes. Stir in dill and season to taste with pepper.

Baked Chickpea Casserole

Makes 6 generous portions

This dish combines the soluble fibres of oat bran and chickpeas, delivering enough for the entire day. You'll notice that at first the oat-bran sauce is very thick, but the spinach will thin it out, and then baking will thin it further. Use as a side dish or add diced ham or turkey breast to make it a main course.

3 tablespoons skimmed milk
175g/6oz oat bran, finely
ground into flour
2 teaspoons cumin powder
2 teaspoons chilli powder

275g/10oz frozen chopped
spinach, thawed
1 green pepper, chopped
2 spring onions, thinly sliced
450g/1lb tin chickpeas

Preheat oven to 190°C/375°F/gas mark 5.

In a large saucepan, slowly bring milk, oat bran, and 400ml/14fl oz water to the boil, stirring constantly with a wooden spoon. When the sauce has thickened, stir in cumin and chilli powders and spinach. Mix until well blended—the sauce will be very thick, but it will thin out in the oven.

Mix in pepper, spring onions and chickpeas and turn into a shallow ovenproof dish. Bake for 15 minutes or until hot.

Chickpea, Garlic, and Thyme Purée

Makes 6 to 8 servings

Here's a welcome alternative to mashed potatoes as an accompaniment to virtually any main course.

4 tablespoons olive oil
1 onion, finely chopped
2 carrots, finely chopped
6 cloves garlic, crushed
2×450g/16oz tins chickpeas,
   drained and rinsed

1 teaspoon dried thyme
Skimmed milk
Pepper

In a medium-sized saucepan heat olive oil, and add onion, carrots, and garlic. Cover and simmer gently for 3 to 4 minutes, or until onion begins to soften.

Add chickpeas, 100ml/4fl oz water, and thyme. Cover and simmer for 20 minutes more. Purée in a food processor or blender. If mixture is too thick, thin with skimmed milk, season to taste with pepper.

Black Bean Cakes

Makes 6 servings

Black beans have a distinctive flavour that really comes through in this dish. You can use the cakes as a side dish, as I prefer, or as a main course if you're in the mood for a vegetarian meal. I like to make the cakes quite spicy, with lots of Tabasco and chilli powder. When using it as a main dish, you may wish to hold back a bit on the spices.

150g/5oz fresh tomatoes, chopped
100g/4oz green chillies
3 tablespoons chopped fresh coriander or parsley
1 tablespoon lemon juice
Tabasco
275g/10oz freshly cooked black beans

25g/1oz oat bran
1 teaspoon ground cumin
1 teaspoon chilli powder
1 spring onion, sliced
Pepper
1-2 tablespoons olive oil
Additional oat bran
Low-fat yogurt

In a small mixing bowl combine tomatoes, green chillies, coriander, and lemon juice. Season to taste with Tabasco and chill until ready to serve.

In a food processor or blender, purée black beans. Mix with oat bran, cumin, chilli powder, and spring onions; season to taste with pepper. Shape mixture into 5cm/2in cakes.

In a large frying pan, preferably nonstick, heat olive oil. Dip each cake on both sides in oat bran and sauté for 2 to 3 minutes per side. Serve with chilled tomato-and-chilli sauce and yogurt.

Black Beans and Rice Medley

Makes 4 to 6 servings

This recipe provides another example of how foods can be combined to give a full protein complement with no meat at all. Beans and rice are a staple in many parts of the world. But if you'd really enjoy some meat, you can add some diced smoked ham or turkey to round out the dish.

1 tablespoon corn or olive oil
½ small onion, finely chopped
1 green pepper, finely chopped
1 stalk celery, finely chopped
¼ teaspoon garlic powder
½ teaspoon thyme

200g/7oz parboiled long-grain rice
275g/10oz cooked black beans
3 tablespoons chopped fresh parsley or 4 teaspoons dried
Pepper

In a medium-sized saucepan heat oil and stir-fry onion, pepper, and celery for 1 minute. Cover saucepan and cook for 3 to 4 minutes, or until vegetables have softened. Add garlic and thyme and stir in rice. Add 450ml/¾ pint water and bring to the boil. Cover pan and simmer gently for 10 minutes.

Add black beans, stir, cover, and simmer for another 10 minutes or until rice is cooked through. Stir in parsley and season to taste with pepper.

Creole Red Beans and Rice

Makes 4 to 6 servings

This is a staple food throughout Louisiana, especially down around New Orleans. It's a tasty side dish along with some blackened salmon (see page 179).

2 tablespoons olive or corn oil
2 spring onions, thinly sliced
1 green pepper, finely chopped
1 stalk celery, finely chopped
½ teaspoon garlic powder

½ teaspoon dried thyme
¼ teaspoon cayenne
450g/1lb tin red kidney beans
with liquid
200g/7oz long-grain rice

In a medium-sized saucepan, heat oil and stir in spring onions, pepper, and celery. Sauté for 2 to 3 minutes.

Add garlic, thyme, and cayenne, and sauté for 10 seconds. Add kidney beans and their liquid. Stir in rice and 350ml/12fl oz water. Cover and simmer gently for 20 minutes. Remove cover and fluff up with a fork.

Braised Red Kidney Beans and Cabbage

Makes 8 servings

This dish can be served as a side dish or main course, or you can serve it in place of salad, before the meal. If you use it as a main course, you might want to add some diced lean ham. Any way you choose, it's a treat.

397g/14oz tin no-salt-added tomatoes, chopped
1 ½ teaspoons caraway seeds
½ medium cabbage, shredded
225g/8oz fresh mushrooms, sliced

2 × 450g/1lb tins kidney beans, drained
Pepper

In a large saucepan, bring tomatoes and caraway seeds to the boil. Add cabbage and mushrooms, cover and simmer, stirring every now and then, for 30 minutes or until cabbage is tender but still has some crunch to it. Add beans and simmer, uncovered, for 15 minutes longer. Season to taste with pepper.

Red Bean Stir-Fry

Makes 4 servings

Red beans are a particular favourite in Louisiana cookery, while water chestnuts are a staple in Chinese stir-fry dishes. In this dish the water chestnuts provide a fine textural contrast to the soft beans. While you can rely entirely on the corn oil, the sesame oil offers a distinct flavour.

1 tablespoon soya sauce
½ teaspoon ground ginger
½ teaspoon sugar
2 teaspoons sesame oil
1 teaspoon corn oil
225g/8oz tin sliced water
*   chestnuts*

1 garlic clove, crushed
450g/1lb tin red kidney beans,
*   well rinsed and drained*
2 spring onions, thinly sliced

In a small dish, whisk together soya sauce, ginger, and sugar until well combined.

In a large frying pan, preferably nonstick, heat sesame and corn oils, over high heat. When very hot, add water chestnuts and garlic and stir-fry for 30 seconds, stirring constantly. Add beans and stir-fry for another 1 to 2 minutes, or until very hot. Add spring onions and soya-sauce mixture and simmer for another minute.

Red Beans with Garlic and Ginger

Makes 6 servings

The flavours of both garlic and ginger are well absorbed by beans. Fresh ginger is preferable to powdered in this recipe, but for a real taste treat, look for crystallized ginger to use in this and other recipes calling for ginger.

1 tablespoon olive oil
1 tablespoon finely chopped
fresh garlic
1 tablespoon finely chopped
fresh ginger or 2 teaspoons
powdered ginger

100ml/4fl oz chilli sauce
575g/1¼ lb cooked red beans
Pepper

In a medium-sized saucepan, heat oil. When very hot, add garlic and ginger. Cover and simmer very gently for 3 minutes, making sure garlic does not burn.

Add chilli sauce and beans. Cover and simmer gently for 30 minutes. Season to taste with pepper.

Barbecued Kidney Beans

Makes 6 servings

These beans will give you a taste of the Old West. Serve with grilled hamburgers made with lean beef.

1 small onion, finely chopped
250ml/8fl oz ketchup
2 tablespoons Worcestershire
  sauce
2 teaspoons sugar

2 tablespoons red wine or cider
  vinegar
2×450g/1lb tins red kidney
  beans, **drained and rinsed**

In a medium-sized saucepan, combine onion, ketchup, 3 table-spoons water, Worcestershire sauce, sugar, and vinegar. Bring to the boil, then simmer for 5 minutes. Add kidney beans and simmer, uncovered, for 10 minutes or until heated through.

Split Pea and Potato Purée

Makes 6 servings

The combination of peas and potatoes yields a particularly rich and satisfying soup. Enjoy it as a prelude to dinner or along with a sandwich.

200g/7oz green split peas
450g/1lb potatoes, peeled and
    halved
1 clove garlic, crushed
1 tablespoon olive oil

½ teaspoon rosemary
Pepper
6 tablespoons finely chopped
    fresh parsley, optional

In a medium-sized saucepan, bring peas, potatoes, garlic, oil, rosemary, and 750ml/1¼ pints water to the boil. Cover, then simmer gently for 45 minutes, or until peas are tender. Check on peas every now and then to see if they need a bit more water.

Purée through a food mill or in a food processor. Season to taste with pepper and fold in parsley if you wish.

Pease Pudding

Makes 8 servings

Pease porridge hot, pease porridge cold, pease porridge in the pot nine days old. Kids used to chant the words, but how many of us know what pease porridge is? Nothing more than a purée of cooked split peas, baked and set by egg whites, this dish can be eaten hot or cold. It only improves when kept in the fridge for a while. Season to your taste. But I guarantee this thickened pudding won't stay around anywhere near nine days.

450g/1lb green split peas
1 carrot, finely chopped
1 onion, finely chopped
1 celery stalk, finely
  chopped
2 egg whites

1 teaspoon dried spices or
  herbs according to your
  taste, such as marjoram,
  thyme, mint, dill, and/or
  parsley
Pepper

Place peas, carrot, onion, and celery in a large saucepan. Cover with 1.75 litres/3 pints water. Bring to the boil, reduce to a simmer, and cook gently, covered, for 45 minutes.

Preheat oven to 180°C/350°F/gas mark 4.

Drain peas through a colander, reserving liquid for another soup if you wish. Purée peas and vegetables in a food processor, blender, or food mill, and blend in egg whites. Add herbs or spices and pepper according to taste.

Bake in a 1.25 litres/2¼ pint ovenproof dish for 45 minutes.

French Bean Casserole

Makes 8 servings

Just about all the bean recipes in this book can be made with combinations of beans in the way this casserole uses them. For taste, texture,
and visual appeal, the more kinds of beans the better.

350g/12oz cooked chickpeas
*350g/12oz cooked red kidney
  beans*
*350g/12oz cooked white kidney
  or haricot beans*
*150g/5oz stoned black olives,
  chopped*
*250ml/8fl oz no-salt-added
  tomato sauce*

½ teaspoon garlic powder
½ teaspoon thyme
2 tablespoons olive oil
*6 tablespoons chopped fresh
  basil or parsley*
Pepper

Preheat oven to 180°C/350°F/gas mark 4.

Place the chickpeas and beans in an ovenproof dish about
23×33cm/9×13in. Add the black olives, and toss together.

In a small mixing bowl combine tomato sauce, garlic, thyme,
olive oil, and basil; season to taste with pepper. Toss this mixture
with the beans and olives; bake uncovered for 20 minutes.

Mixed Beans and Squash

Makes 6 servings

While vegetables of all sorts contribute some soluble fibre and a significant amount of insoluble fibre, any dish's soluble-fibre content can be boosted tremendously by adding some beans. If you cannot get summer squash, you can substitute marrow or use more courgettes.

2 tablespoons olive oil
1 onion, finely chopped
1 red pepper, finely chopped
150g/5oz each cooked or rinsed
* and drained tinned*
* chickpeas, red beans, and*
* white beans*
250ml/8fl oz no-salt-added
* tomato sauce*

½ teaspoon celery seed
1 small courgette, cut into
* 2.5cm/1in dice*
1 small yellow summer squash,
* cut into 2.5cm/1in dice*
Pepper

In a large saucepan, heat olive oil and sauté onion and red pepper for 3 to 4 minutes. Add beans, tomato sauce, and celery seed. Cover the pan and simmer gently for 15 minutes.

Stir in squash and simmer, covered, for 5 minutes more, or until the squash is just tender; season to taste with pepper.

Mixed Vegetable and Bean Pudding

Makes 6 to 8 servings

This recipe will perk up even the most jaded tastebuds.

2 tablespoons olive oil
100g/4oz chopped onions
275g/10oz freshly cooked or
   450g/1lb tin borlotti beans,
   drained and rinsed
100ml/4fl oz no-salt-added
   tomato sauce

50g/2oz oat bran
275g/10oz frozen mixed
   vegetables, thawed
3 egg whites

Preheat oven to 180°C/350°F/gas mark 4. Lightly grease a 13 × 23cm/5 × 9in loaf tin and set aside.

In a medium-sized frying-pan heat olive oil and sauté onions for 5 minutes or until softened; stir continuously so they do not burn.

Transfer onions, beans, tomato sauce, and oat bran to a food processor or blender and mix until smooth. Transfer mixture to a bowl and fold in the vegetables.

Beat egg whites until stiff, then fold them into the bean-and-vegetable mixture. Pour mixture into prepared loaf tin, then cook for 1 hour. Spoon out servings.

Persian Rice and Lentils

Makes 6 to 8 servings

In this dish, rice cooks gently for so long that a wonderful crust develops on the bottom of the pot and gives the dish a deep, rich flavour. It's worth cleaning the dish at the end.

1 tablespoon corn oil	**¼ teaspoon saffron**
100g/4oz lentils	**½ teaspoon honey**
2 carrots, finely chopped	**Pepper**
200g/7oz long-grain rice	

Spread oil on the bottom of a medium-sized saucepan. Add lentils, carrots, rice, saffron, honey, and 750ml/1¼ pints water. Season to taste with pepper.

Very slowly bring liquid to the boil, cover, and simmer very gently until rice and lentils have absorbed all the liquid; this may take as long as 35 minutes. You can eat this dish at once, or you can form a rice crust in the following way.

Place a damp towel over the rice and lentils, cover again, and cook very slowly and gently for 30 minutes more or until the bottom crusts. When you serve the rice, simply break this dried crusty rice into the tender kernels for a wonderfully interesting textural contrast.

Sweet Swedish Lentils

Makes 6 servings

Preparing tasty dishes needn't mean elaborate preparation. This simple dish goes well with any number of meat or fish entrées.

200g/7oz lentils	*2 tablespoons white wine*
2 tablespoons brown	*vinegar*
sugar	*Pepper*

In a medium-sized saucepan bring lentils and 750ml/1¼ pints water to the boil. Cover, then simmer gently for 30 minutes or until lentils are tender. Check the lentils every now and then to see if they need a bit more water.

Meanwhile, simmer sugar with vinegar until sugar is dissolved. When lentils are tender, stir in sugar-and-vinegar mixture and simmer for 5 minutes. Season to taste with pepper.

Sweet-and-Sour Lentils

Makes 8 to 10 servings

Planning a picnic or barbecue party? This dish is a natural for any outdoor get-together.

450g/1lb brown lentils
175ml/6fl oz white wine
  vinegar
250ml/8fl oz tomato juice
1 pickled gherkin, chopped
1 stalk celery, chopped

1 teaspoon sugar
1 teaspoon prepared mustard
2 tablespoons Worcestershire
  sauce
6 tablespoons chopped parsley

Pick through lentils and rinse, place them in a saucepan, and cover with water. Bring to the boil, reduce to a simmer, and cook gently, partially covered, for 25 minutes or until lentils are just tender. Be sure they remain covered with water while they are cooking. Drain lentils and place in a mixing bowl.

Combine all remaining ingredients in a blender or food processor and purée until smooth. Toss this dressing over warm lentils. Cover, and marinate at room temperature for 2 hours.

Artichoke and Chicken Risotto

Makes 4 to 6 servings

Rice bran comes through to give a creamy texture to this delicious dish.

1 tablespoon olive oil
1 small onion, thinly sliced
225g/8oz artichoke hearts,
  chopped
397g/14oz tin no-salt-added
  tomatoes
200g/7oz long-grain parboiled
  rice

350g/12oz boneless, skinless
  chicken breast, cut into
  2.5cm/1in cubes
*25g/1oz rice bran, **finely ground***
Pepper
3 tablespoons Parmesan cheese,
  optional

In a medium-sized saucepan, heat olive oil. Add sliced onions and stir-fry for 2 to 3 minutes. Add artichoke hearts and tomatoes, rice, and 450ml/¾ pint water. Simmer, covered, for 10 minutes.

Add chicken and simmer for 5 minutes more, then stir in rice bran and simmer for 2 minutes. Season to taste with pepper and serve lightly sprinkled with cheese if you wish.

Mushroom Risotto

Makes 4 to 6 servings

If you've never experienced it, you'll be surprised at the creamy texture of risotto. That creaminess comes from slowly simmering and stirring short-grain white rice for 35 minutes. This recipe takes a short cut, using the more common long-grain rice, without the need for continuous stirring. It's the rice bran mixed with the Parmesan cheese that gives the dish its marvellous creaminess.

1 tablespoon olive oil
225g/8oz fresh mushrooms,
 finely chopped
200g/7oz long-grain parboiled
 rice

15g/ ½ oz rice bran, **finely**
 ground
3 tablespoons grated Parmesan
Pepper

In a medium-sized saucepan heat olive oil. Add mushrooms and 2 tablespoons of water; cover and simmer gently for 10 minutes.

Add rice to the pan, along with 600ml/1 pint water. Cover and simmer gently for 15 to 20 minutes, or until rice is just tender. Stir in rice bran and Parmesan and cook for a minute or so longer. Season with pepper to taste and serve immediately, or the mixture will dry out and turn sticky.

Risotto Milanese

Makes 4 servings

A classic risotto calls for long simmering of short-grain rice to provide the characteristic creaminess. This recipe is made with long-grain rice, to which is added rice bran to give it the creaminess of the classic dish.

1 tablespoon olive oil
3 tablespoons finely chopped
  onion
⅛ teaspoon saffron
200g/7oz long-grain parboiled
  rice

20g/¾ oz rice bran
Pepper
3 tablespoons grated Parmesan

In a medium-sized saucepan heat olive oil and sauté onion for 1 minute. Add saffron and rice and cover with 600ml/1 pint water. Bring to the boil, reduce to a simmer, and cook gently, covered, for 17 minutes.

Stir in rice bran and cook a minute or so more, or until rice is just tender to the bite. Season to taste with pepper and serve with Parmesan.

Indian Rice Pilaff

Makes 6 servings

The sweetness of sugar and the zing of curry combine to give you a tasty side dish to serve with grilled salmon or beef.

1 tablespoon corn or olive oil
1 small onion, finely chopped
1 teaspoon sugar
1 teaspoon curry powder
200g/7oz parboiled long-grain rice

15g/½ oz rice bran
75g/3oz raisins
Pepper

In a medium-sized saucepan, heat oil and sauté onion for 2 to 3 minutes. Stir in sugar and curry powder and sauté for 30 seconds more.

Add rice, rice bran, and 600ml/1 pint water. Bring to the boil, reduce to a simmer, and cook gently, covered, for 12 minutes.

Stir in raisins, cover, and cook for 3 to 5 minutes longer, or until rice is just tender. Season to taste with pepper, fluff up with a fork, and serve.

Rice and Carrot Pancakes

Makes 4 servings or 2 pancakes each

You can enjoy this cholesterol-lowering dish as an appetizer along with some low-fat yogurt or as a potato-substitute side dish.

25g/1oz rice bran
400g/14oz long-grain rice
150g/5oz grated carrot

2 spring onions, thinly sliced
½ teaspoon curry powder
2 egg whites

In a blender or food processor, finely grind rice bran. Add cooked rice, carrots, spring onions, curry powder, egg whites, and 100ml/4fl oz water. Process until you have formed a thick mixture.

With your hands, shape the mixture into 8 patties. Heat a lightly-greased nonstick frying pan. When hot, sauté the pancakes for about 4 minutes per side.

Chilled Tomato and Vegetable Purée

Makes 6 servings

During the hot summer months, try this chilled dish along with a turkey sandwich for a complete meal without heating the kitchen.

50g/2oz rice bran
2 spring onions
1 red or green pepper, chopped
1 cucumber, peeled and
   chopped

3 tablespoons red wine vinegar
550ml/18fl oz V8 juice
450ml/¾ pint tomato juice
1 clove garlic
Pepper

Purée all ingredients in a food processor or blender. Cover and chill, preferably overnight.

Spring Onion and Oat-Bran Johnnycakes

Makes 4 servings (or 8 to 10 cakes)

This dish makes an unusual breakfast, a nice lunch, or a side dish for dinner. For the main meal of the day I like the cakes with thick slices of lean ham and some vegetables.

65g/2 ½ oz maize flour
50g/2oz oat bran
1 teaspoon baking powder
2 spring onions, thinly sliced

Tabasco
2 egg whites
1-2 tablespoons corn oil

Blend maize flour and oat bran with baking powder; stir in spring onions. (This can all be done in a food processor.)

Bring 250ml/8fl oz water to the boil and mix it into the flour and bran mixture; season to taste with Tabasco. Transfer mixture to a bowl.

Whip egg whites until stiff and fold into batter.

Heat a nonstick frying pan until very hot, or heat 1 tablespoon of the oil in a cast-iron frying pan. When oil is hot, drop in 3 tablespoons of batter for each johnnycake and cook for 2 minutes per side. If needed, use the remaining oil to fry the other johnnycakes.

Carrot and Potato Pancakes

Makes 6 servings or 12 to 14 pancakes

Traditionally, potato pancakes are quite greasy. The recipe as it stands calls for only one to two tablespoons of corn oil.

4 carrots, peeled and grated	*50g/2oz oat bran*
2 medium potatoes, peeled and grated	*Salt and pepper to taste*
2 egg whites	*1-2 tablespoons corn oil*

Preheat oven to 120°C/250°F/gas mark ½.

In a large mixing bowl combine carrots, potatoes, egg whites, and oat bran. Season to taste with salt and pepper.

Heat 1 tablespoon of the oil in a large frying pan, preferably nonstick. While oil is heating up, shape carrot-and-potato mixture into little pancakes, using about 4 tablespoons of the mixture for each one. When shaping the pancakes squeeze the mixture tightly.

Sauté the pancakes, over low heat, for 5 minutes on the first side. With a spatula, turn the pancakes over, pressing down hard to flatten them out, and sauté for 10 minutes on the second side. Repeat procedure until all the carrot mixture has been used up. If you are working in several batches, put the first pancakes on a baking tray and place them, uncovered, in the oven to keep warm.

Barley and Green Pea Medley

Makes 6 to 8 servings

To get the onions nice and soft, cover the frying pan while sautéing. This tip applies to many other recipes as well.

1 tablespoon olive oil
1 onion, finely chopped
200g/7oz pearl barley
275g/10oz frozen peas,
preferably petit pois, thawed

Pepper
6 tablespoons Parmesan cheese

In a medium-sized saucepan heat olive oil, add onion and simmer, covered, for 5 minutes or until very soft. If onion begins to burn or stick, add a few teaspoons of water and continue to cook.

Add barley and stir around for 30 seconds. Add 600ml/1 pint water and simmer gently, partially covered, for 20 minutes. Add peas and pepper to taste, and simmer for another 5 minutes or until barley is just tender to the bite. Stir in Parmesan and serve immediately.

Chinese Fried Barley

Makes 4 servings

Traditional Chinese fried rice uses leftover rice. You can make this dish to use up any leftover barley you may have from time to time. You can make it either as a side dish or main course.

1 tablespoon corn oil
450g/1lb cooked pearl barley
200g/7oz petit pois, thawed
225g/8oz very lean ham, cut
   into 1cm/½ in cubes
3 egg whites

2 spring onions, thinly sliced
2 tablespoons low-salt soya
   sauce
3 tablespoons rice or white
   wine vinegar
Pepper

Heat oil in a large frying pan over high heat. When very hot, add barley, peas, and ham, and stir-fry for 1 minute. Add egg whites, spring onions, soya sauce, and vinegar, and stir-fry for 1 to 2 minutes more or until egg whites have formed long, thin white threads and the mixture is very hot. Season to taste with pepper and serve immediately.

Mushroom Barley Pilaff

Makes 6 servings

Many of us get stuck in a rut when it comes to side dishes. Here's a wonderful alternative you and your family will love.

15g/½ oz dried mushrooms
2 tablespoons olive oil
1 red pepper, finely chopped
4 cloves garlic, crushed

275g/10oz fresh mushrooms,
*   finely chopped*
200g/7oz pearl barley
Pepper

Soak dried mushrooms in 450ml/¾ pint hot water for 30 minutes or until rehydrated. Cut off any parts of mushrooms that remain tough. Chop mushrooms and reserve soaking water.

In a medium-sized saucepan heat olive oil. When hot, add red pepper, garlic, fresh mushrooms, and chopped mushrooms. Sauté for about 3 to 4 minutes.

Add barley to 900ml/1½ pints water. Cover and simmer gently for 25 minutes. Look at the barley every now and again to make sure bottom is not burning and that you have enough liquid to cover. If water level has gone down before barley is tender, simply add 100ml/4fl oz more and simmer until done.

SAUCES AND TOPPINGS

Onion Raisin Sauce
Tomato Sauce
Tomato, Chickpea, and
  Turkey Sauce

Curried Split Pea Sauce
Seasoned Crumbs

Onion Raisin Sauce

Makes 4 servings

A meal of gammon, Brussels sprouts, and mashed potatoes sounds pretty good. But when you ladle this sauce over the gammon and sprouts you have a real taste treat. The sauce alone provides half the soluble fibre you need for the day.

1 tablespoon corn oil
1 onion, thinly sliced
1 tablespoon wine vinegar
40g/1 ½ oz raisins
15g/ ½ oz rice bran

100ml/4fl oz skimmed milk
   mixed with 350ml/12fl oz
   chicken stock or water
Pepper

In a medium-sized saucepan heat oil, add onion and stir-fry for 1 to 2 minutes. Add vinegar, raisins, and a couple of tablespoons of water. Cover and simmer gently for 10 to 12 minutes, or until onions are very soft. Be sure to stir every now and then to make sure the onions are not sticking; if they are, add a tablespoon or two of water.

Stir in rice bran, add milk and stock, and bring to the boil. Stir and simmer for 2 minutes; season to taste with pepper.

Additions

This makes a thin sauce—good when served over something that will absorb it, like mashed potatoes. To thicken it, one can add 1 scant teaspoon guar gum and whisk it in, off heat (the texture works, although the flavour of the guar gum always comes through). One could also purée the sauce to make it thicker.

Tomato Sauce

Makes about 1.15 litres/2 pints

The characteristic sweetness of truly authentic Italian tomato sauce usually comes from the plum tomatoes. Here you can get the sweetness, along with extra body and soluble fibre from apple fibre. Use the sauce with pastas of all sorts.

2 tablespoons olive oil
2 onions, finely chopped
4 cloves garlic, crushed
2 carrots, finely chopped
1kg/2 ¼ lb tinned plum
  tomatoes

2 tablespoons chopped fresh or
  1 teaspoon dried basil
½ teaspoon oregano
Pepper
15-25g/ ½ -1oz apple fibre

In a large saucepan heat olive oil, stir in onions, garlic, and carrots, and sauté for 3 to 4 minutes. Add tomatoes and their juice. Add herbs and pepper, cover, and simmer gently for 45 minutes.

Purée sauce in a blender or food processor. Add apple fibre to thicken it. (Add the maximum amount for a thicker sauce.) Return sauce to the saucepan and simmer 5 minutes.

Tomato, Chickpea, and Turkey Sauce

Makes enough for 6 servings of pasta

This sauce offers a tasty change of pace for pastas. It works particularly
well with pasta shapes that can catch the sauce, such as fusilli, penne, and
shells.

2 tablespoons olive oil
1 onion, thinly sliced
1 clove garlic, crushed
1.5 litres/2 ¾ pints no-salt-
added tomato sauce
275g/10oz cooked or drained
tinned chickpeas

225g/8oz finely-chopped
turkey breast
4 tablespoons chopped basil
leaves
3 tablespoons chopped black
olives
Pepper

In a large frying pan, heat olive oil. When hot, sauté onion for 3
to 4 minutes. Stir in garlic and sauté for 30 seconds more. Add
tomato sauce and chickpeas and cover. Simmer for 10 minutes.

Add remaining ingredients, cover, and simmer 10 minutes
longer.

Curried Split Pea Sauce

Makes 4 servings

You don't have to work very hard to prepare Indian-style curry. As you see, three ingredients do the trick. Pour the curried peas over rice and serve with a piece of grilled fish. Or, if you prefer, you can add the fish to the peas during the last ten minutes of cooking. I enjoy a glass of beer with Indian food.

90g/3 ½ oz green split peas   *1 teaspoon garlic powder*
1 tablespoon curry powder

Bring split peas and 750ml/1¼ pints water to the boil. Simmer for 15 minutes, skimming off froth as it rises to the top. Add curry and garlic powders and continue to simmer, partially covered, for 30 to 45 minutes or until peas are soft. Serve over cooked rice or barley.

Seasoned Crumbs

Makes about 275g/10oz

I prepare a lot of oven-fried foods since everyone in my family enjoys them. We save a lot of fat cooking chicken, scallops or shrimp by coating them with seasoned crumbs, and then baking. Chicken takes about 30 minutes in a preheated oven; seafood requires less time. You can make a batch of the crumbs to keep on hand whenever the mood for oven-fried foods strikes.

100g/4oz oatmeal
100g/4oz oat bran
40g/1 ½ oz maize flour

1 tablespoon dry mixed herbs, or ¾ teaspoon each dried basil, oregano, marjoram, thyme, sage, and rosemary
2 egg whites

Preheat oven to 200°C/400°F/gas mark 6.

In a mixing bowl combine oatmeal, bran, maize flour, and dried herbs. Mix in egg whites and, with your hands, squeeze the mixture together as best you can. The egg whites should help the herbs adhere to the oat mixture, which should fall together now in small clumps; some of the mixture will remain dusty-looking.

Transfer mixture to a 25×36cm/9×13in baking dish and cook for 30 to 45 minutes, stirring every 15 minutes or so or until the mixture smells toasty and looks slightly yellow.

CEREALS, PANCAKES, BREADS, AND MUFFINS

Toasted Rice and Oat-Bran Hot Cereal
Barley Maple Porridge
Crunchy Cereal Topping
Date and Raisin Bars
Three-Grain Pancakes
Oat-Bran and Rice-Fibre Pancakes
Oatmeal and Oat-Bran Bread
Barley Bread
Onion Rye and Oat-Bran Bread
Oatmeal Sweet Bread
Boston Brown Bread
Pumpkin Bread
Jalapeño Cornbread
Banana Date-Nut Bread
Fruit Bread
Italian Dinner Rolls

Bannocks
Baking-Powder Biscuits
English Muffin Loaf
Oatcakes
Oat-Bran and Apple-Fibre Muffins
Cranberry Oat-Bran Muffins
Orange Oat-Bran Muffins
Lemon-Glazed Oat-Bran Muffins
Maple and Spice Oat-Bran Muffins
Strawberry Muffins
Gingerbread Rice-Bran Muffins
Raisin Rice-Bran Muffins
Orange Rice-Bran Muffins
Blueberry Muffins
Apple-Fibre Raisin Muffins

Toasted Rice and Oat-Bran Hot Cereal

Makes 1 serving

Here's a way to get even more soluble fibre into your breakfast bowl than from oat bran alone. But don't limit this to the morning; it makes a great evening snack as well.

3 tablespoons oat bran	*40g/1 ½ oz raisins*
3 tablespoons rice bran	*Brown sugar*
3 tablespoons skimmed milk,	*Ground cinnamon*
mixed with 175ml/6fl oz	

Heat a small saucepan. When hot, add oat bran and rice bran and stir continuously with a wooden spoon for about a minute, or until the oat bran gives off an aroma of popcorn. Be careful to stir all the time as you do this or some of the bran could burn.

Add milk and water and raisins and bring to the boil. Simmer for 1 minute, and serve, dusted with brown sugar and cinnamon.

Barley Maple Porridge

Makes about 1 breakfast serving

I get bored pretty quickly with breakfast cereals, and this mixture offers a nice alternative. Try it with some fresh fruit in season.

40g/1 ½ oz pearl barley	**1 tablespoon maple syrup**
2 tablespoons rice bran	**1 tablespoon skimmed milk**
Pinch of ground cinnamon	

In a saucepan bring barley, 250ml/8fl oz water, rice bran, cinnamon, and maple syrup to the boil. Lower heat, cover the pot, and simmer gently for 10 minutes. Add milk and continue to simmer for 5 to 10 minutes more, or until enough liquid has evaporated to suit your taste and the barley is tender. You'll have to watch the pot as it simmers, once the milk is added, as the barley and milk tend to boil over.

Crunchy Cereal Topping

Makes about 100g/4oz

This is a delightful topping to sprinkle over yogurt. You get the sweetness and crunch of the rice bran with the extra flavour of the spices. This mixture also makes a delicious cold cereal or dry snack. Even desserts can be a wonderful source of soluble fibre.

100g/4oz *rice bran*
2-4 tablespoons honey

**½ teaspoon each of cinnamon
  and cardamom**
¼ teaspoon ground nutmeg

Preheat oven to 180°C/350°F/gas mark 4.

In a mixing bowl combine rice bran, honey according to taste, and spices. Mix with a fork or your fingers.

Transfer mixture to a 23×33cm/9×13in ovenproof dish and bake for 5 to 10 mninutes. Watch the mixture carefully, as it tends to burn quickly.

Date and Raisin Bars

Makes 16 to 20 squares

Just take a quick glance at the ingredients list on fruit bars and you'll know you don't want to buy them. Here's a healthy alternative that's low in fat and high in fibre.

350g/12oz oatmeal
50g/2oz rice bran
½ teaspoon bicarbonate of
soda
½ teaspoon cinnamon
100g/4oz raisins

100g/4oz chopped stoned dates
175ml/6fl oz skimmed milk
6 tablespoons honey
3 egg whites
100g/4oz sugar

Preheat oven to 180°C/350°F/gas mark 4. Lightly grease a 23cm/9in baking tin.

In a mixing bowl, with a fork or whisk, blend oatmeal, rice bran, bicarbonate of soda, cinnamon, raisins, and dates.

In a bowl combine milk and honey.

Beat egg whites until almost stiff. Slowly, about a tablespoon at a time, add the sugar to the whites and continue to beat until stiff and glossy.

Stir the liquid ingredients into the dry ones. Fold half the egg whites into the oatmeal batter to lighten and moisten it, then add the other half. Spoon the batter into the prepared baking tin, and bake for 35 minutes or until a toothpick, when inserted into the centre of the batter, comes out dry. It will be easier to cut this into squares if you leave the fruit bars overnight at room temperature.

Three-Grain Pancakes

Makes about eight 7.5cm/3in pancakes

All three grains supply soluble fibre and together make delicious and unusual pancakes.

40g/1 ½ oz maize flour
40g/1 ½ oz oat bran
20g/ ¾ oz rice bran
2 tablespoons sugar

½ teaspoon baking powder
300ml/ ½ pint boiling water
2 egg whites

Preheat a nonstick frying pan.

In a food processor or blender, combine maize flour, oat bran, rice bran, sugar, and baking powder, and process until smooth. Add boiling water and transfer batter to a mixing bowl.

Beat egg whites until stiff, and fold them into the batter.

Drop 2-3 tablespoonsful of batter for each pancake into the hot frying pan, and cook for about 4 minutes on each side.

Oat-Bran and Rice-Fibre Pancakes

Makes about 12 pancakes

As with all baked goods, this recipe tastes best if you first beat the egg whites and then fold them into the batter, rather than just combining all the ingredients. That little extra step makes all the difference in the world.

175g/6oz oat bran
25g/1oz rice bran
2 tablespoons sugar
2 teaspoons baking powder

250ml/8fl oz skimmed milk
100ml/4fl oz water
2 egg whites

Preheat a nonstick frying pan.

In a mixing bowl, combine oat bran, rice bran, sugar, and baking powder. Combined skimmed milk and water, and stir into the dry ingredients. Beat egg whites until stiff and then fold them into the batter.

Drop 2-3 tablespoonsful of batter for each pancake into the hot pan, and cook 5 minutes on each side. These pancakes need to be cooked thoroughly or they will taste very heavy.

Oatmeal and Oat-Bran Bread

Makes one 10×20cm/4×8in loaf

Try this bread, either fresh from the oven or toasted for breakfast one morning. Spread with a little honey, jam, or marmalade, it's a wonderful treat.

225g/8oz quick-cooking oatmeal	**1 teaspoon salt**
	1 teaspoon sugar
50g/2oz oat bran	**2 tablespoons corn oil**
15g/½ oz sachet yeast	**About 200g/7oz flour**

Soak oatmeal and bran for 2 hours in 350ml/12fl oz water. The mixture will be sticky-looking.

Dissolve yeast in 3 tablespoons warm water.

With a wooden spoon, beat, as best you can, salt, sugar, and 1 tablespoon of the oil into the oatmeal mixture. Stir in the dissolved yeast and water and mix as well as possible

Add a third of the flour to the mixture; if too stiff to stir, switch to your hands and squeeze the oatmeal and flour together; this is messy but it all works out well in the end. Try to work in another third of the flour.

Then sprinkle 2 tablespoons of the flour onto a lightly floured work surface. Turn the shaggy oatmeal-and-flour mixture onto the flour and knead the flour into the dough. Knead for 6 or 7 minutes, working in as much of the remaining flour as you need to make a smooth but not too stiff dough. Set dough in a lightly oiled mixing bowl; cover surface of dough with some oil so that it does not crust. Cover the bowl with a damp towel and set in a warm, draft-free place. It should take about 1½ to 2 hours for this bread to rise. When sufficiently risen, the dough will look puffy, although it will never double in volume.

Punch dough down and knead for a minute more. Lightly grease a 10×20cm/4×8in loaf tin. Shape the dough into a sausage and place in the prepared tin. Cover with a damp cloth and leave to rise for 45 minutes.

Preheat oven for 20 minutes to 200°C/400°F/gas mark 6. Bake for 45 to 50 minutes. To test if the bread is done, insert a knife into the centre; it should come out dry. Or you could turn the bread out from its tin and tap the bottom; if it sounds hollow, the bread is done. This loaf will always look pale and whitish, because of the colour of the oatmeal.

Barley Bread

Makes two 13×23cm/5×9in loaves

Granted, baking with yeast takes a bit of time and effort, but it's worth it.

2×15g/½ oz sachet yeast
450ml/¾ pints reserved pearl
  barley cooking water, if you
  have it, or use warm water
1 tablespoon molasses

2 tablespoons corn oil
400g/14oz cooked pearl barley
100g/4oz oat bran
1 teaspoon salt
About 800g/1 ¾ lb flour

In a large bowl, dissolve the yeast in the warm barley water or plain water.

With a wooden spoon stir the molasses and oil, cooked barley, oat bran, and salt into the yeast. Stir in 450g/1lb of the flour.

Sprinkle 50g/2oz flour onto your work surface and put the dough onto it; sprinkle 50g/2oz flour on top. With your hands work the flour in. Again sprinkle flour on the board and over the dough and knead it in.

Then sprinkle flour onto the work surface. Dip your hands in the remaining flour and knead the dough for 6 or 7 minutes, dipping your hands lightly in flour if the dough becomes too sticky, but using only what is necessary.

Place dough in a lightly oiled mixing bowl; cover surface of dough with a little oil so that it does not crust, then cover the bowl with a damp towel and set in a warm, draft-free place. It should take about 2 hours for this bread to rise; when sufficiently risen, the dough will look puffy and should have doubled in volume.

Punch dough down and knead for a minute more. Lightly grease two 13×23cm/5×9in loaf tins. Divide the dough in half, shape each loaf into a sausage, and place in the prepared loaf tins. Cover the loaf tins with a damp cloth and leave to rise for 45 minutes.

Preheat oven for 15 minutes to 190°C/375°F/gas mark 5. Bake loaves for 1 hour. To test if the bread is done, insert a knife or toothpick into the centre; it should come out dry. Or you could turn the loaves out of the tins and tap the bottoms; if they sound hollow, they are done. These loaves will always look pale, because of the colour of the oat bran.

Oatmeal Sweet Bread

Makes one 13×23cm/5×9in loaf

Quick to make, but long to bake!

100g/4oz oat bran
150g/5oz oatmeal
150g/5oz flour
50g/2oz sugar
½ teaspoon bicarbonate of
soda

1 teaspoon baking powder
¼ teaspoon powdered
cardamom
170g/6oz raisins
450ml/¾ pint buttermilk
3 egg whites

Preheat oven to 180°C/350°F/gas mark 4. Lightly grease a 13×23cm/5×9in loaf tin.

In a mixing bowl, whisk together oat bran, oatmeal, flour, sugar, bicarbonate of soda, baking powder, cardamom and raisins; mix thoroughly.

Stir buttermilk into the dry ingredients.

Beat egg whites until stiff. Fold half of the egg whites into the batter to lighten it, then fold in the remaining half. Spoon the batter into the prepared loaf tin.

Bake for 1 hour and 20 minutes. Turn bread out from tin onto a cake rack and thoroughly cool to room temperature before slicing.

Onion, Rye, and Oat-Bran Bread

Makes two 13×23cm/5×9in loaves

Breads made with oat bran typically do not rise very well because oats lack the gluten that makes wheat rise. The answer is to use flour which has extra gluten added to it. No doubt baking bread takes a lot of time and effort, but the aroma filling the house makes it worth while.

4×15g/½ oz sachets yeast
4 tablespoons honey
450ml/¾ pint low-fat yogurt
2 teaspoons each caraway, dill,
   and fennel seed
275g/10oz rye flour

1 tablespoon corn oil
65g/2½ oz finely-chopped
   onion
350g/12oz oat bran
1½ teaspoons salt
About 275g/10oz flour

Dissolve yeast in 250ml/8fl oz warm water in a large bowl and stir in honey.

In a small saucepan, gently heat yogurt with seeds until warm to the touch. Stir this into yeast and stir in the rye flour. Cover mixture and let it sit in a warm place for 2 hours, or until it becomes spongy; this process will help the bread rise later on.

Meanwhile, heat corn oil in a small frying pan and sauté onion until brown; remove and set aside.

With a wooden spoon stir into the dough the oat bran, a tablespoon at a time, then stir in salt and cooked onions.

Sprinkle 50g/2oz flour onto a work surface and put the rye-and-oat-bran dough on it; sprinkle 50g/2oz flour on top of the dough. With your hands work the flour in. Then sprinkle more flour underneath the dough and over the top and knead in the flour, working the dough for about 5 minutes. If the dough becomes sticky, keep on dusting its surface and your hands with more flour. Do not overdo this step, however, as you want to keep the dough moist.

Place dough in a lightly oiled mixing bowl; cover surface of dough with some oil so that it does not crust. Then cover the bowl with a damp towel and set in a warm, draft-free place to rise, for about 2 hours. The dough will look puffy but will not have doubled in volume.

Punch dough down and knead for a minute. Lightly grease two 13×23cm/5×9in loaf tins. Divide the dough in half and shape each loaf into a sausage. Place in the prepared loaf tins. Cover with a damp cloth again and leave to rise for 1 hour longer.

Preheat oven to 190°C/375°F/gas mark 5 for 20 minutes before you bake the bread.

Spray the tops of the loaves lightly with water and set in oven. Bake for 1 hour, spraying the tops with more water every 20 minutes. To test if the bread is done, insert a knife or toothpick into centre; it should come out dry. Or you could turn the loaves out of the tins and tap the bottoms; if they sound hollow, they are done. These loaves will look greyish because of the colour of the rye flour and oat bran.

Boston Brown Bread

Makes one 23cm×9in square loaf

This hearty bread goes especially well with stews and casseroles. Don't be shy about dipping the bread into sauce to get every last drop.

150g/5oz flour
225g/8oz oat bran
65g/2½oz maize flour
1 teaspoon each baking powder
  and bicarbonate of soda

450ml/¾ pint buttermilk
6 tablespoons golden syrup
6 tablespoons molasses

Preheat oven to 180°C/350°F/gas mark 4. Lightly grease a 23cm/9in square tin and set on one side.

In a big bowl, whisk together flour, oat bran, maize flour, baking powder, and bicarbonate of soda. Stir in buttermilk, syrup, and molasses; mixture will be wet. Turn mixture into the prepared tin and cover tightly with foil. Place the tin in a larger one. Fill the larger one with enough hot water to come three-quarters of the way up the sides of the tin filled with batter.

Bake for 1½ hours. Leave the bread to cool in the tin before cutting into squares.

Pumpkin Bread

Makes one 10×20cm/4×8in loaf

Pumpkin bread provides a wealth of vitamin A in the form of beta carotene, and this is an unusual way of using a small quantity of cooked pumpkin.

170g/6oz raisins, soaked in warm water for 15 minutes
150g/5oz cooked pumpkin, puréed
200g/7oz brown sugar
Few drops vanilla essence
2 tablespoons corn oil

225g/8oz oat bran
½ teaspoon baking powder
¼ teaspoon bicarbonate of soda
¼ teaspoon each ground allspice and cloves
3 egg whites

Preheat oven to 180°C/350°F/gas mark 4. Lightly grease a 10×20cm/4×8in loaf tin.

In a mixing bowl or food processor, blend the pumpkin purée, three-quarters of the brown sugar, vanilla, and oil; mix until well combined. Drain the raisins and stir in.

In another large mixing bowl, whisk together the oat bran, baking powder, soda, and spices until thoroughly mixed.

Blend the wet ingredients into the dry ones; the batter will be somewhat dry.

Beat the egg whites until stiff, gradually adding the remaining brown sugar. Fold this into the batter and spoon the batter into the prepared loaf tin.

Bake for 50 to 55 minutes; cool in the tin for 10 minutes before turning out the loaf.

Jalapeño Cornbread

Makes about 16 servings

Some call it Southwestern cooking, others refer to it as Santa Fe cuisine. Whatever the term used, interesting combinations of sweet and spicy ingredients mark this new approach to cooking, which has become very popular in American restaurants. Give this hearty bread a try. Beating and folding in the egg whites rather than simply mixing them into the batter makes the bread lighter.

65g/2 ½ oz maize flour
65g/2 ½ oz plain flour
50g/2oz oat bran
25g/1oz rice bran or apple fibre
2 teaspoons baking powder
½ teaspoon bicarbonate of soda
200ml/7fl oz low-fat buttermilk mixed with 100ml/4fl oz water

1 tablespoon vegetable oil
2 tablespoons minced jalapeño peppers
75g/3oz frozen sweetcorn kernels, thawed
3 egg whites

Preheat oven to 200°C/400°F/gas mark 6. Lightly grease a 20cm/8in square baking tin.

In a large bowl, stir together maize flour, plain flour, brans, baking powder, and soda.

In a small mixing bowl, combine buttermilk and water, vegetable oil, jalapeño pepper, and sweetcorn. Stir into the dry ingredients and mix thoroughly. Beat egg whites until stiff and fold gently into the batter. Pour into the prepared tin and bake for 25 minutes. Cool in tin for 10 minutes before serving.

Banana Date-Nut Bread

Makes one 10×20cm/4×8in loaf

Oat bran is a natural for a dense, satisfying bread such as this one. With this recipe in mind, save very ripe bananas and store them in the freezer until you're ready to use them.

2 very ripe bananas, puréed (this should measure 250ml/8fl oz)	**75g/3oz stoned dates, chopped**
	50g/2oz chopped walnuts
	225g/8oz oat bran
90g/3 ½ oz sugar	**2 teaspoons baking powder**
Few drops vanilla essence	**½ teaspoon ground cinnamon**
2 tablespoons corn oil	**3 egg whites**

Preheat oven to 180°C/350°F/gas mark 4. Lightly grease a 10×20cm/4×8in loaf tin.

In a mixing bowl or food processor, blend puréed bananas with half the sugar, vanilla, and oil; mix until well combined. Stir in dates and nuts.

In another large mixing bowl, whisk together oat bran, baking powder, and cinnamon until thoroughly mixed.

Blend the wet ingredients into the dry ones.

Beat egg whites until stiff, gradually adding the remaining sugar; fold into the batter and spoon the batter into the prepared loaf tin.

Bake for 50 to 55 minutes; cool in pan for 10 minutes before turning out.

Fruit Bread

Makes 2 oval loaves

This delicious, not-too-sweet bread can be made with any kind of dried fruit.

15g/½ oz sachet yeast
450ml/¾ pint warm skimmed
    milk
50g/2oz sugar
2 tablespoons corn oil
350g/12oz dried fruit, such as
    raisins or prunes or apricots
    cut into 1cm/½ in pieces

225g/8oz oat bran
1 teaspoon salt
About 450g/1lb flour
Honey

In a large mixing bowl, dissolve yeast in warm milk. With a wooden spoon stir sugar, oil, dried fruit, oat bran, and salt into the yeast and milk. Stir in half the flour.

Sprinkle a little flour on a work surface and put the batter on it; sprinkle some more flour on top. With your hands work the flour in, squeezing and working the dough as best you can; it will be sticky and hard to manage.

Then sprinkle a little more flour onto the working board. Dip your hands in the remaining flour and knead the dough for 6 to 7 minutes, dipping your hands lightly in flour if the dough becomes too sticky. You may not use all of the flour.

Place dough in a lightly oiled mixing bowl. Cover surface of dough with some oil so that it does not crust, then cover the bowl with a damp towel and set in a warm, draft-free place. It should take about 2 hours for this bread to rise; when sufficiently risen, the dough will look puffy, although it never will double in volume.

Punch dough down and knead for a minute more. Lightly grease a baking tray. Divide the dough into 2 parts and shape into two oval loaves, about 15cm/6in long. Put the loaves on the baking tray, cover with a damp cloth again, and leave to rise for 45 minutes to 1 hour.

Preheat oven for 20 minutes to 190°C/375°F/gas mark 5. Bake for about 1 hour. To test if the bread is done, insert a knife or toothipick into centre; it should come out dry. Or you could turn the bread over and tap the bottom; if it sounds hollow, it is done. While the bread is still warm, lightly brush the top with honey to give a glaze and a softer texture.

Italian Dinner Rolls

Makes 12 to 16 rolls

While you can use either rice bran or apple fibre in this recipe, it comes
out a lot better if you use half of each. The apple fibre gives a bit of
sweetness and the rice bran offers a nutty flavour. Both supply a lot of
soluble fibre. I really don't think these rolls need any margarine at all.

15g/½ oz sachet yeast
250ml/8fl oz warm water (not
  hotter than 115°F)
2 tablespoons sugar
100g/4oz rice bran or half rice
  bran and half apple fibre
65g/2 ½ oz wholewheat flour

About 275g/10oz plain flour
1 teaspoon salt
1 teaspoon crumbled rosemary
  or oregano
100ml/4fl oz low-fat yogurt
2 tablespoons olive oil

Place yeast in a small mixing bowl, add warm water, and stir with
a fork. Add sugar, and set aside.

   Although this is not a crucial step, if you toast the rice bran first,
the flavour of the bread will be nice and toasty; you should not,
however, toast the apple fibre. To give the rice bran a nutty
popcorn flavour, heat a large frying pan over high heat, add the
bran and stir continuously, with a wooden spoon, for 2 minutes
or until it smells nutty; it will turn a deeper shade of brown.

   Transfer rice bran to a bowl, and add wholewheat flour and
225g/8oz plan flour, salt, and rosemary. With a whisk or fork, stir
to combine thoroughly.

   To the yeast in the small mixing bowl add yogurt and olive oil.
Add the liquid to the dry ingredients and beat with a wooden
spoon until dough is combined.

   Turn dough onto a well-floured board and knead about 25g/1oz
flour into the dough. Knead the dough for about 8 minutes,
dusting your hands with flour as you work. Try not to incorporate
all the remaining flour into the dough, so that the dough remains
as moist as possible. Turn dough around in an oiled bowl and
cover well. Set in a draught-free place and let the dough rise for
1½ hours.

   Punch dough down and divide into 12 or 16 pieces. Roll each
piece into a neat ball and set on a baking tray; cover and leave to
rise for 40 to 45 minutes.

Preheat oven to 200°C/400°F/gas mark 6. Bake rolls for 18 to 20 minutes. Remove from oven and cool 20 minutes before eating.

Bannocks

Makes about 24

This simple recipe is baked on a griddle, but is more like a biscuit than a griddlecake. You can serve bannocks for breakfast, lunch, dinner, or snacks. Enjoy them with preserves or honey.

225g/8oz oat bran
350g/12oz oatmeal **finely ground**
*1 teaspoon **bicarbonate of soda***

450ml/¾ pint boiling water
3 tablespoons corn oil
Flour

Preheat a griddle or large nonstick frying pan.

In a mixing bowl, combine oat bran, oatmeal, and bicarbonate of soda. Combine water and oil and stir into the batter, which will be somewhat stiff.

Dip your hands in flour, then take about 2 tablespoons of the dough and pat it into a round, about 5mm/¼in thick.

Cook 10 minutes on each side on low heat; these bannocks need to be cooked thoroughly or they will taste very heavy—their texture should be somewhat like a disgestive biscuit.

Baking-Powder Biscuits

Makes about eighteen 4cm/1½in biscuits

Biscuits like these taste best hot out of the oven. Plan them to give a nice touch to your dinner as well as a lot of soluble fibre. I like mine with honey, but you might prefer to spread on a bit of margarine and let it melt into the hot biscuit.

150g/5oz plain flour   **25g/1oz** apple fibre
1 tablespoon baking powder   **⅛ teaspoon salt**
25g/1oz rice bran   **200ml/7fl oz skimmed milk**

Preheat oven to 230°C/450°F/gas mark 8.

In a mixing bowl, stir together flour, baking powder, rice bran, apple fibre, and salt. Or you could do this in a food processor. Add milk all at once and stir until ingredients are just combined; if you are doing this in a food processor, pulse the machine a few times until dough is combined. If the dough seems a little dry, sprinkle on a tablespoon of water, and work it in.

With lightly floured hands, knead the dough for 30 seconds. Then pat and push it out until it is 1cm/½in thick. With a 4cm/1½in biscuit cutter, cut dough into about 18 rounds. Set rounds on an ungreased baking tray. Bake for 16 minutes or until cooked through.

Variations

To make herbed biscuits, add 1 teaspoon dried herbs of your choice to the dry ingredients, before adding the milk.

To make buttermilk biscuits, use buttermilk instead of the skimmed milk and substitute 2 teaspoons baking powder, mixed with ½ teaspoon bicarbonate of soda.

To make oat-bran biscuits, substitute 50g/2oz oat bran for the rice bran and apple fibre.

English Muffin Loaf

Makes two loaves, 10 slices per loaf

This is an unusual recipe for breakfast. It's particularly good sliced and toasted, with a bit of marmalade or jam.

275g/10oz oat bran
350g/12oz wholewheat flour
150ml/5fl oz nonfat dried milk
2×15g/½ oz sachets yeast
1 tablespoon granulated sugar

½ teaspoon salt
¼ teaspoon bicarbonate of soda
600ml/1 pint warm water
1 tablespoon maize flour

Preheat oven to 200°C/400°F/gas mark 6. In a large mixing bowl combine all ingredients except water and maize flour. Add water and mix thoroughly. Cover with greaseproof paper and leave to rise till double in bulk, about 35 minutes. Lightly grease two 13×23cm/5×9in loaf tins and sprinkle on maize flour so a little sticks to the bottom and sides of the tins. Divide dough and place into the prepared tins. Bake 25 minutes.

Oatcakes

Makes 2 ½ dozen 5cm/2in biscuits

Because these biscuits have so little oil, they tend to harden and dry out rather quickly. Enjoy them right out of the oven, spread with jam or honey.

275g/10oz oatmeal	**2 tablespoons corn oil**
75g/3oz **high-gluten flour**	**6 tablespoons skimmed milk**
25g/1oz oat bran	**4 tablespoons water**
½ **teaspoon salt**	**Flour**

Preheat oven to 180°C/350°F/gas mark 4.

In a food processor or blender combine oatmeal, flour, oat bran, and salt, and mix until oatmeal is somewhat broken up. Transfer dry ingredients to a mixing bowl.

Stir liquid ingredients into the dry ones and knead for 2 minutes. The dough will be somewhat resistant.

On a floured board, with lightly floured rolling pin, roll the dough out until 3mm/⅛in thick. With a 5cm/2in biscuit cutter, cut into rounds. Gather scraps of dough into a ball, roll out the dough, and cut into rounds. Do this until all the dough has been cut out.

Place biscuits on an ungreased baking tray and bake for 45 minutes.

Oat-Bran and Apple-Fibre Muffins

Makes 12 muffins

The French eat croissants for breakfast regularly from the cradle to grave and don't get tired of them. I prefer a bit more variety. Here oat bran and apple fibre combine to deliver more soluble fibre than oat bran alone, and with a nice flavour twist. You can further modify the recipe with some chopped nuts, dried fruit bits, or little pieces of fresh fruit or berries.

225g/8oz oat bran	*350ml/12fl oz skimmed milk*
25g/1oz apple fibre	*75g/3oz raisins*
½ teaspoon bicarbonate of soda	*2 egg whites*
2 tablespoons corn oil	*2 tablespoons white or brown sugar*

Lightly grease 12 muffin tins or use paper baking cases. Preheat oven to 200°C/400°F/gas mark 6.

In a large mixing bowl, combine oat bran, apple fibre, and bicarbonate of soda.

In another mixing bowl, combine oil, milk, and raisins; set aside.

Beat egg whites until stiff, gradually beating in the sugar.

Stir the liquid ingredients into the dry ones, and immediately fold the egg whites into the batter. You should not stir the liquid ingredients into the dry ones before you are ready to fold in the egg whites because the batter will become stiff and it will be hard to work in the egg whites.

Spoon the batter into the prepared muffin tins or baking cases and bake for 18 minutes or until a toothpick inserted in the centre of a muffin comes out clean.

Cranberry Oat-Bran Muffins

Makes 24 muffins

I like these muffins so much that I keep a supply of cranberries in my freezer so I can enjoy them throughout the year, not just during the autumn and winter. Using a food processor to render the oat bran to a flourlike consistency gives the muffins a lighter, cakier texture. You can, of course, cut the recipe in half to make only 12 muffins, but I think you'll like them so much you'll want the full two dozen.

450g/1lb oat bran
75g/3oz granulated sugar
2 tablespoons baking powder
350ml/12fl oz white grape juice
350ml/12fl oz skimmed milk

6 egg whites
3 tablespoons corn oil
100g/4oz fresh or frozen whole
  cranberries
25g/1oz chopped walnuts

Preheat oven to 220°C/425°F/gas mark 7. Combine oat bran, sugar, and baking powder in food processor with large metal blade. Allow the food processor to grind the oat bran as you combine the moist ingredients in a separate bowl or blender. Add whole cranberries to the oat bran in the food processor and pulse the mixture for a few seconds to break up the berries. Combine all ingredients, including chopped walnuts, in a large bowl and mix gently. Pour batter into muffin pans lined with baking cases. Bake 17 minutes. To test if the muffins are ready, pierce with a toothpick; it should come out moist but not wet.

  You don't have to use a food processor for this recipe. Just omit the grinding of the oat bran and cut the cranberries into small pieces with a sharp knife.

Orange Oat-Bran Muffins

Makes 24 muffins

You can create a wide variety of tasty muffins merely by changing the type of liquid used as a sweetener. Here concentrated orange juice, with a little grated orange rind provides an extra zing. You can also use soda water to give additional lightness to any of the recipes for muffins or other baked goods.

This recipe makes two dozen muffins. You can adapt all your oat-bran muffin recipes accordingly, to give you a full week's supply or to allow you to freeze a dozen for future use.

450g/1lb oat bran
50g/2oz chopped walnuts
100g/4oz granulated sugar
2 tablespoons baking powder
3 tablespoons grated orange peel
350ml/12 fl oz concentrated orange juice

350ml/12fl oz skimmed milk
2 tablespoons corn oil
2 tablespoons golden syrup
6 egg whites
Soda water

Preheat oven to 220°C/425°F/gas mark 7. In a large bowl combine oat bran, nuts, sugar, baking powder, and orange peel. Mix all moist ingredients except soda water and blend together with dry ingredients. Add a little soda water and gently fold into batter; not too much, just about a tablespoon or two, and you'll see the batter puff up. Pour batter into muffin tins lined with paper baking cases. Bake 17 minutes. To test if the muffins are ready, pierce with a toothpick; it should come out moist but not wet.

Lemon-Glazed Oat-Bran Muffins

Makes 12 muffins

Here we give oat-bran muffins a little extra touch by way of the glaze topping. You can do the same thing with orange or lime juice for a variety.

275g/10oz oat bran
½ teaspoon bicarbonate of
  soda
200g/7oz sugar
3-6 tablespoons chopped
  walnuts, optional

2 tablespoons corn oil
250ml/8fl oz skimmed milk
6 tablespoons lemon juice
2 egg whites

Lightly grease a 12-cup muffin tin or use paper baking cases. Preheat oven to 200°C/400°F/gas mark 6.

In a large mixing bowl, combine oat bran, bicarbonate of soda, 150g/5oz sugar, and walnuts, if you are using them.

In another mixing bowl, combine oil, milk, 3 tablespoons lemon juice, and 3 tablespoons water.

Beat egg whites until frothy. Gradually beat in the rest of the sugar, and beat until the mixture is stiff and glossy.

Beat the liquid ingredients into the dry ones, and immediately fold the egg-white mixture into the batter. You should not beat the liquid ingredients into the dry ones before you are ready to fold in the egg white mixture. The longer the oat bran sits, the stiffer this batter becomes and the harder it is to work in the egg whites.

Scoop the batter into the prepared muffin tin or baking cases and bake for 18 minutes. Stir together the remaining sugar and 3 tablespoons lemon juice.

When cupcakes are done, poke each one, while still hot, with a toothpick, making about 5 holes in each. Spoon the lemon juice and sugar glaze over the cupcakes while they are still warm. Cool to room temperature.

Maple and Spice Oat-Bran Muffins

Makes 12 muffins

Just a simple thing like changing the sweetening agent and the spices can make an entirely different muffin. Here we've used maple syrup along with allspice, cardamom, cinnamon, and nutmeg, I think you'll really like the result.

250g/9oz oat bran
1 teaspoon baking powder
⅛ teaspoon each ground allspice, cardamom, cinnamon, and nutmeg

50g/2oz chopped walnuts
150g/5oz maple syrup
250ml/8fl oz skimmed milk
2 egg whites

Lightly grease a 12-cup muffin tin or use paper baking cases. Preheat oven to 220°C/400°F/gas mark 6.

In a large mixing bowl, combine oat bran, baking powder, spices, and walnuts.

In another mixing bowl, combine maple syrup and milk.

Beat egg whites until stiff.

Beat the liquid ingredients into the dry ones and immediately fold in the beaten egg whites.

Spoon the batter into the prepared muffin tin or baking cases and bake for 18 minutes.

Strawberry Muffins

Makes 12 muffins

You can use frozen berries in this recipe, but fresh ones make it so much better. For dessert, try the muffins spread with some strawberry jam.

175g/6oz oat bran
50g/2oz apple fibre
1 teaspoon bicarbonate of soda
275g/10oz strawberries, fresh
    or frozen, preferably
    unsweetened

75g/3oz sugar
Skimmed milk, if needed
2 tablespoons corn oil
3 egg whites

Preheat oven to 220°C/425°F/gas mark 7. Line 12 muffin cups with paper baking cases or lightly grease with oil.

In a large mixing bowl or in the food processor, combine oat bran, apple fibre, and bicarbonate of soda. Stir until thoroughly mixed.

Place in a blender or food processor half the strawberries with the sugar and purée until smooth. Measure the strawberry purée; if it does not measure 250ml/8fl oz, add enough skimmed milk to bring it to that level. Dice remaining strawberries.

In a small mixing bowl combine the strawberry purée and oil, and stir this into the dry ingredients to combine thoroughly. Stir in the chopped strawberries.

Beat egg whites until stiff and fold them into the batter. Spoon the batter into the prepared baking cases and bake for 20 minutes.

Gingerbread Rice-Bran Muffins

Makes 12 muffins

Because there's more soluble fibre per 25g/1oz in rice bran than in oat bran, you can combine the rice bran with flour to make muffins that are a potent source of soluble fibre. This recipe shows how you can use the rice bran like flour by finely grinding it in a food processor or blender.

75g/3oz rice bran **finely ground**
90g/3 ½ oz plain wholewheat flour
1 ½ **tablespoons baking powder**
¾ teaspoons each ginger and cinnamon

40g/1 ½ oz raisins
100ml/4fl oz hot water
225g/8oz molasses
2 tablespoons corn oil
2 egg whites

Preheat oven to 220°C/425°F/gas mark 7. Mix dry ingredients, including raisins, together in a large bowl. Mix moist ingredients in a blender and then add to dry ingredients. Pour batter into muffin tins lined with paper baking cases. Bake 15 to 17 minutes.

Raisin Rice-Bran Muffins

Makes 12 muffins

While oat-bran muffins have been my breakfast staple for years, it's nice to have a change now and then. These muffins provide all the soluble fibre I need from the rice bran and apple fibre. As with all muffin recipes, you can use 2 egg whites beaten until fluffy and then folded into the batter.

50g/2oz rice bran
25g/1oz apple fibre
90g/3 ½ oz flour
¾ teaspoon bicarbonate of soda
50g/2oz sugar

90g/3 ½ oz raisins
175ml/6fl oz buttermilk mixed with 100ml/4fl oz water
2 tablespoons corn oil
2 tablespoons honey
2 egg whites

Preheat oven to 220°C/425°F/gas mark 7. Line 12 muffin cups with paper baking cases or grease lightly with oil

In a large mixing bowl or a food processor, combine oat bran, apple fibre, flour, bicarbonate of soda, and sugar. Stir until thoroughly mixed; stir in the raisins.

In a small mixing bowl, combine buttermilk and water, oil, honey, and egg whites. Stir this into dry ingredients and mix thoroughly. Spoon batter into the prepared baking cases and bake for 18 minutes or until a toothpick inserted into the centre of a muffin comes out clean.

Orange Rice-Bran Muffins

Makes 12 muffins

Rice bran can be used to boost the soluble-fibre content of practically any recipe. There are some recipes that just don't lend themselves to oat bran in place of wheat flour. In these you can just add some rice bran.

150g/5oz plain flour
65g/2 ½ oz rice bran
50g/2oz sugar
1 tablespoon fresh grated orange zest

1 tablespoon baking powder
2 tablespoons corn oil
300ml/ ½ pint orange juice
2 egg whites

Lightly grease 12 muffins cups or use paper baking cases. Preheat oven to 200°C/400°F/gas mark 6.

In a large mixing bowl, combine flour, rice bran, sugar, orange zest, and baking powder.

In another mixing bowl, combine oil, orange juice, and beaten egg whites.

Beat the liquid ingredients into the dry ones, and scoop the batter into the prepared muffin cups or baking cases. Bake for 18 to 20 minutes.

Blueberry Muffins

Makes 12 muffins

I think you're going to really like the combination of oat bran with maize flour. And the blueberries—heaven! These taste especially good hot out of the oven, so plan to make them on a leisurely Sunday morning.

175g/6oz oat bran
150g/5oz maize flour
40g/1 ½ oz sugar
1 tablespoon baking powder
250ml/8fl oz skimmed milk

2 tablespoons corn oil
50g/2oz blueberries, fresh or
   frozen
3 egg whites

Preheat oven to 220°C/425°F/gas mark 7. Line 12 muffin cups with paper baking cases or grease lightly with oil.

In a large mixing bowl or in the food processor, combine oat bran, maize flour, sugar, and baking powder. Stir until thoroughly mixed.

In a small mixing bowl combine milk and oil, and stir into the dry ingredients to combine thoroughly; stir in the blueberries.

Beat egg whites until stiff and fold them into the batter. Spoon the batter into the prepared muffin cups or baking cases and bake for 20 minutes.

Apple-Fibre Raisin Muffins

Makes 12 muffins

Now and then I like to take a break from oat bran muffins, and then I turn to muffins made with another source of soluble fibre. Apple fibre in these muffins and in almost any recipe adds a bit of sweetness and a whole lot of fibre.

50g/2oz apple fibre
150g/5oz flour
150g/5oz brown sugar
½ teaspoon bicarbonate of soda
2 teaspoons baking powder

½ teaspoon ground cinnamon
150g/5oz raisins
250ml/8fl oz skimmed milk
250ml/8fl oz buttermilk
3 egg whites

Lightly grease a 12-cup muffin tin or use paper baking cases. Preheat oven to 200°C/400°F/gas mark 6.

In a large mixing bowl, combine apple fibre, flour, sugar, bicarbonate of soda, baking powder, and cinnamon; whisk thoroughly. Add raisins and stir in milk and buttermilk.

Beat egg whites until stiff and fold them into the batter, working in one-third of the egg whites at a time.

Scoop the batter into the prepared muffin tin or baking cases and bake for 20 minutes.

DESSERTS AND SWEETS

Apple Sauce Oat-Bran Cake
Courgette Cake
Mocha Torte
Cranberry Orange Cake
Ginger Cake
Rum Torte
Carrot Cake
Apricot Cake
Dried-Fruit Oatmeal Crisp
Apple-Fibre and Oatmeal
  Cookies
Gingersnaps
Honey Oatmeal Drop
  Cookies

Oatmeal 'Smacks'
Chocolate, Chocolate
  Brownies
Prune and Date Bars
Raspberry Fool
Mocha Pudding
Berry Pudding
Indian Barley Pudding
Rice Pudding
Fruit and Fibre Jelly
Chocolate Milkshake
Orange Guar
Orange Guar Smoothie

Apple Sauce Oat-Bran Cake

Makes one 23×33cm/9×13in cake

It's really easy to convert just about any cake into a heart-healthy dessert. First replace half the flour with oat bran or apple fibre. Next use egg whites instead of whole eggs. Finally, replace the butter or margarine with corn oil. This is a terrific snack cake that needs no topping at all.

200g/7oz plain flour
150g/5oz oat bran **or** apple fibre
400g/14oz granulated sugar
150g/5oz raisins
3 tablespoons chopped walnuts
1 teaspoon bicarbonate of soda
1 tablespoon baking powder
¾ teaspoon ground cinnamon

¼ teaspoon ground cloves
¼ teaspoon ground allspice
350g/12oz apple sauce
3 tablespoons golden syrup
3 tablespoons corn oil
4 egg whites
100ml/4fl oz soda water

Preheat oven to 180°C/350°F/gas mark 4. Lightly grease a baking tin 23×33cm/9×13in. Mix all dry ingredients in a large bowl, then mix together all moist ingredients except soda water. Blend moist ingredients with the dry. Add soda water and gently fold into batter; you'll see the batter puff up. Bake about 60 minutes. Test with toothpick to determine whether cake is ready.

Sprinkle top of cake with half-and-half mixture of cinnamon and granulated sugar, if you wish.

Courgette Cake

Makes one 23cm/9in square cake

Courgette must be one of the easiest vegetables to grow in the world; everyone I know who's ever planted it has had a bumper crop. If you become a courgette farmer, or know someone who is, you'll be looking for ways to use it. Here's a perfect application.

65g/2 ½ oz flour	*450g/16oz grated courgettes*
25g/1oz rice bran, **finely ground**	*150g/5oz raisins*
50g/2oz apple fibre	*450ml/ ¾ pint skimmed milk*
1 teaspoon bicarbonate of soda	*5 egg whites*
½ teaspoon allspice	*200g/7oz sugar*

Preheat oven to 190°C/375°F/gas mark 5. Lightly grease a 23cm/9in square tin.

In a large mixing bowl, whisk together flour, rice bran, apple fibre, bicarbonate of soda, and allspice, and mix thoroughly. Stir in courgettes and raisins.

Blend milk into the dry ingredients and mix well.

Beat egg whites until stiff. Slowly and gradually add the sugar to the egg whites and continue to beat until thick and glossy.

Fold half of the egg whites into the batter to lighten it, then fold in the remaining half. Spoon the batter into the prepared cake tin.

Bake for 1 hour; cool in tin to room temperature before slicing into squares. This is a very moist cake.

Mocha Torte

Makes one 23cm/9in torte

Here's a way to enjoy chocolate flavour without chocolate fat.

100g/4oz oat bran
40g/1 ½ oz flour
6 tablespoons unsweetened
  cocoa
½ teaspoon bicarbonate of
  soda

2 teaspoons powdered coffee
5 egg whites
200g/7oz sugar

Preheat oven to 180°C/350°F/gas mark 4. Lightly grease a 23cm/9in tin.

In a mixing bowl, combine oat bran, flour, cocoa, bicarbonate of soda, and coffee.

With an electric mixer, beat egg whites until frothy. Tablespoon by tablespoon, beat sugar into the egg whites until the egg whites become very stiff and shiny.

Sprinkle one-quarter of the dry ingredients onto the egg whites and, with a spoon, fold them into the egg whites. Add one-quarter more of the dry ingredients and fold, and so on until the ingredients are completely homogenized. When you are folding the whites and dry ingredients together, work swiftly but gently, taking care to deflate the egg whites as little as possible. Spoon the batter into the prepared tin.

Bake for 30 minutes. Lower heat to 160°C/325°F/gas mark 3 and bake for 15 minutes longer. Remove from oven and cool in cake tin for 15 minutes. With a knife, loosen edges and gently loosen cake from bottom. Turn upside down onto a cake rack and cool. When completely cool, serve as is or dusted with icing sugar.

Cranberry Orange Cake

Makes one 20×10cm/8×4in loaf

Remember that it's best to spread your intake of soluble fibre throughout the day rather than having it all at one time. Cakes like this one make it easy and delicious to do just that. A muffin in the morning and some cake at night—not a bad way to stay heart-healthy!

100g/4oz cranberries, frozen or
  fresh
200g/7oz sugar
2 tablespoons grated orange
  peel
175g/6oz oat bran

25g/1oz apple fibre
2 teaspoons baking powder
2 teaspoons vanilla
175ml/6fl oz orange juice
2 tablespoons corn oil
3 egg whites

Preheat oven to 180°C/350°F/gas mark 4. Lightly grease a 20×10cm/8×4in loaf tin.

With a sharp knife or in a food processor, chop cranberries with 50g/2oz sugar and blend in orange peel; set aside.

In a large mixing bowl, whisk together oat bran, apple fibre, and baking powder, and mix thoroughly.

In another smaller mixing bowl, combine vanilla, orange juice, 250ml/8fl oz water, and the oil. Blend the liquid ingredients into the dry ones.

Whip egg whites until stiff. Slowly and gradually add the remaining sugar to the egg whites and continue to beat until very stiff and glossy.

Fold half of the mixture into the batter to lighten it, then fold in the remaining half. Spoon the batter into the prepared loaf tin.

Bake for 1 hour; cool in tin for 10 minutes before turning onto a cake rack.

Ginger Cake

Makes two 20cm/8in cakes

Beating the egg whites helps make this cake light and airy. The flavour is wonderful and the orange glaze a perfect topper.

25g/1oz rice bran
25g/1oz apple fibre
62g/2 ½ oz flour
1 teaspoon baking powder
1 teaspoon ground ginger
½ teaspoon grated orange zest
250ml/8fl oz skimmed milk
  mixed with 100ml/4fl oz
  water

5 egg whites
175g/6oz sugar

OPTIONAL ORANGE GLAZE
2 tablespoons frozen orange-
  juice concentrate, thawed
6 tablespoons icing sugar

Preheat oven to 180°C/350°F/gas mark 4. Lightly grease two 20cm/8in cake tins.

In a mixing bowl, combine rice bran, apple fibre, flour, baking powder, ginger, and orange zest. Stir milk and water into the dry ingredients and mix to form a wet batter-like dough.

With an electric mixer, beat egg whites until frothy. Tablespoon by tablespoon, beat sugar into the egg whites, and beat until the egg whites become very stiff and shiny.

With a spoon, fold half of the egg whites into the bran batter, then fold in the remaining half. When you are folding the whites into the batter, work swiftly but gently, taking care not to deflate the egg whites too much; they are what will lighten the cake.

Bake for 30 minutes. Lower heat to 160°C/325°F/gas mark 3 and bake for 15 minutes longer. Remove from oven and cool in cake tin for 15 minutes. With a knife, loosen edges and gently loosen cake from bottom. Turn upside down on a cake rack and cool. When completely cool, serve as is or dusted with icing sugar.

If you wish, mix the ingredients for the glaze and spread half on top of one cake. Set second cake on top of first and spread remaining glaze over the top; some may drip down the sides of the cake, and that will make it look pretty. Let glaze set for half an hour before serving.

Rum Torte

Makes one 23cm/9in torte, or 8 servings

Puréed beans give this torte a body and flavour reminiscent of chestnuts. Use freshly cooked beans rather than tinned ones for the best results.

200g/7oz cooked or tinned
  *haricot beans, **drained and***
  rinsed
175g/6oz sugar
4 tablespoons rum

Few drops vanilla essence
15g/½ oz apple fibre
5 egg whites
3-4 tablespoons fruit jam,
  optional

Preheat oven to 180°C/350°F/gas mark 4. Lightly grease a 23cm/9in round cake tin.

In a blender or food processor, purée beans, 50g/2oz sugar, and the rum and vanilla until smooth. Add apple fibre and purée. If the mixture seems dry, add 2 to 3 tablespoons water to make a thick batter.

Beat egg whites until stiff, then gradually beat in the remaining sugar. Fold gently into the bean-and-fibre mixture. Spoon into prepared cake tin and bake for 50 minutes, or until a toothpick, when inserted into centre of cake, comes out dry.

Serve warm. Or, when cake has cooled to room temperature, cut it into two thin horizontal layers with a serrated knife. Spread the bottom layer with the jam and place the second layer on top. Leave to rest for a couple of hours before serving.

Carrot Cake

Makes one 23cm/9in square cake

Oat bran is a natural for heavy cakes such as a carrot cake. Port is my favourite choice, though sherry works well also, to give the cake a real flavour boost. This cake is a winner.

225g/8oz raisins	*200g/7oz brown sugar*
3 tablespoons port or sherry	*100ml/4fl oz corn oil*
150g/5oz oat bran, processed	*3 tablespoons skimmed milk*
into flour	*3 tablespoons golden syrup*
100g/4oz plain flour	*Few drops vanilla essence*
1 tablespoon baking powder	*6 egg whites*
2 teaspoons ground cinnamon	*275g/10oz grated fresh carrots*

Preheat oven to 200°C/400°F/gas mark 6. Lightly grease a 23cm/9in square baking tin.

In a small mixing bowl, soak raisins in port and set aside.

In a mixing bowl, sift together oat bran, flour, baking powder, and cinnamon.

Place in another bowl brown sugar, oil, milk, golden syrup, vanilla and egg whites, and mix with an electric mixer for a minute or two. Add carrots to the liquid mixture, then stir in the flour mixture, then the raisins and port. Pour mixture into prepared baking tin and bake for 40 to 45 minutes, or until a toothpick, when inserted in centre of cake, comes out dry. Let cool to room temperature, then cut into squares.

Apricot Cake

Makes one 23cm/9in square cake

This cake recipe calls for half high-gluten flour and half apple fibre. You can turn virtually any cake recipe into a source of soluble fibre simply by replacing half the flour with apple fibre. Spoon a bit of apricot jam over the cake as a topping.

200g/7oz chopped stoned dates
450g/16oz tin of apricots,
   drained and coarsely
   chopped
200g/7oz sugar
4 tablespoons corn oil

2 teaspoons bicarbonate of
   soda
350ml/12fl oz apricot nectar
50g/2oz apple fibre
150g/5oz flour
4 egg whites

Preheat oven to 180°C/350°F/gas mark 4. Lightly grease 23cm/9in square tin.

In a mixing bowl, combine dates and apricots. Add half the sugar, the oil, and bicarbonate of soda. Heat nectar to boiling point and pour over ingredients; let mixture cool.

Beat egg whites until stiff. Slowly and gradually add the remaining sugar to the egg whites and continue to beat until very stiff and glossy.

With a wooden spoon beat apple fibre and flour into the fruit mixture.

Fold half of the egg whites into the batter to lighten it, then fold in the remaining half. Spoon the batter into the prepared cake tin.

Bake for 1 hour or until a toothpick inserted into centre of cake comes out clean. Cool in tin to room temperature before slicing into squares.

Dried-Fruit Oatmeal Crisp

Makes 6 servings

This is delicious and flavourful, and even tastier with a topping of some sort—a few dollops of frozen yogurt, perhaps.

175g/6oz dried apricots	**TOPPING**
175g/6oz dried stoned prunes	**2 tablespoons brown sugar**
100g/4oz raisins	**20g/¾ oz** rolled oats
100g/4oz dried figs, chopped	**25g/1oz** oat bran
¼ teaspoon cinnamon	**15g/½ oz** apple fibre
¼ teaspoon cloves	**3 tablespoons chopped walnuts,**
100ml/4fl oz port or red wine	**optional**
2 tablespoons apple fibre	**1 tablespoon corn oil**

Preheat oven to 180°C/350°F/gas mark 4.

Combine all the fruit in a 23cm/9in square baking tin. In a small mixing bowl, combine cinnamon, cloves, wine (or substitute orange juice or water if you wish) and apple fibre. Mix until well combined, and blend with the dried fruit.

In another mixing bowl, combine sugar, oats, oat bran, apple fibre, and nuts if desired, and sprinkle this on the dried fruit. Drizzle the oil over the top and bake for 35 to 40 minutes, or until fruit has softened somewhat and topping has browned.

Apple-Fibre and Oatmeal Cookies

Makes 3 dozen

I got this recipe from some friends. When my wife and children tried these cookies, they couldn't believe they're good for you.

65g/2 ½ oz plain flour	*150g/5oz seedless raisins*
25g/1oz apple fibre	*50g/2oz chopped nuts*
½ teaspoon bicarbonate of	*2 egg whites*
soda	*200g/7oz brown sugar*
¼ teaspoon salt, optional	*100ml/4fl oz oil*
175g/6oz quick-cooking	*100ml/4fl oz skimmed milk*
oatmeal	*1 teaspoon vanilla essence*

Preheat oven to 180°C/350°F/gas mark 4. Sift together flour, apple fibre, bicarbonate of soda, cinnamon, and salt, if you wish. Stir in oatmeal, nuts, and raisins. Combine egg whites, sugar, oil, milk, and vanilla. Add to flour mixture and mix well. Drop by tablespoons onto a lightly greased baking tray. Bake 10 to 12 minutes.

Gingersnaps

Makes 24 to 28

Crisp gingersnaps, along with a glass of cold skimmed milk will wake up the child in you. If no one's looking, you might even want to dunk the cookies in the milk. But remember what happens if you hold the cookie in the milk too long; timing is everything!

100g/4oz oat bran	½ teaspoon ground cloves
100g/4oz flour	3 tablespoons corn oil
1 teaspoon baking powder	3 tablespoons golden syrup
¾ teaspoon each ground	2 egg whites
cinnamon and ginger	90g/3½ oz sugar, white or brown

Preheat oven to 190°C/375°F/gas mark 5. Lightly grease two baking trays.

In a mixing bowl, with a fork or whisk blend oat bran, flour, baking powder, cinnamon, ginger, and cloves.

In a small bowl combine oil and golden syrup.

Beat egg whites until almost stiff. Slowly add sugar to the whites and continue to beat until stiff and glossy.

Stir the liquid ingredients into the dry ones—the two won't homogenize at all and will remain crumbly, but that is all right. Stir half of the egg whites into the oat-bran batter to lighten and moisten it, then stir in the other half. Stir until the oat bran and spice mixture and egg whites are well mixed.

Drop the batter by teaspoonsful onto the prepared baking trays and bake for 10 to 12 minutes. If you are using two racks, switch the trays around halfway during baking. Keep your eye on the cookies as they will burn quickly.

Honey Oatmeal Drop Cookies

Makes 22 5cm/2in cookies

Here's a variation on oatmeal cookies with added soluble fibre from oat bran. They're on the chewy side and not too sweet. Depending on your tastes, you might want to add a bit more sugar.

50g/2oz oat bran
175g/6oz oatmeal
40g/1 ½ oz flour
¼ teaspoon baking powder
⅛ teaspoon allspice

2 tablespoons corn oil
2 egg whites
1 teaspoon vanilla essence
3 tablespoons honey
75g/3oz brown sugar

Preheat oven to 180°C/350°F/gas mark 4. Lightly grease two baking trays.

In a large mixing bowl combine oat bran, oatmeal, flour, baking powder, and allspice.

In a blender or food processor, combine oil, egg whites, vanilla, honey, and brown sugar. Blend these liquid ingredients into the dry ones.

By tablespoons, drop the batter onto the prepared baking trays and bake for 12 to 14 minutes.

Oatmeal 'Smacks'

Makes 16 squares

These morsels got their name because they are so delicious one needs to 'smack' one's lips after eating them. This revised 'healthy' version is still good enough to 'smack' one's lips!

100g/4oz oat bran, finely ground into flour	*75g/3oz chopped stoned dates*
65g/2 ½ oz plain flour	*4 egg whites*
50g/2oz oatmeal	*2 tablespons corn oil*
90g/3 ½ oz brown sugar	*1 teaspoon vanilla essence*
2 teaspoons baking powder	*2 egg whites*
	90g/3 ½ oz brown sugar

Preheat oven to 180°C/350°F/gas mark 4. Lightly grease a 20cm/8in baking tin.

In a food processor or electric mixer combine oat bran, flour, oatmeal, brown sugar, and baking powder; stir in chopped dates.

In a small mixing bowl combine the 4 egg whites, oil, and vanilla. Add to the dry ingredients. With your hands mix and squeeze the ingredients together until you have formed a dough that just holds together.

Pat the dough into the prepared baking tin. Beat the 2 egg whites until stiff, then gradually add the brown sugar, a tablespoon at a time, until all of it has been incorporated. Spread this over the dough and bake for 45 minutes. Cool to room temperature and cut into 16 squares.

Chocolate, Chocolate Brownies

Makes about 18 brownies

One of my favourite recipes in *The 8-Week Cholesterol Cure* is my oat-bran brownies. I've enjoyed them for years to satisfy my chocolate cravings. Here's another version I think you'll like. You'll find they're easier to cut into squares if left to sit overnight. That is, if you can stay away from them that long!

225g/8oz oat bran	*4 tablespoons corn oil*
12 tablespoons unsweetened cocoa	*1 tablespoon vanilla essence*
½ teaspoon bicarbonate of soda	*6 egg whites*
100ml/4fl oz skimmed milk	*200g/7oz brown sugar*
	200g/7oz white sugar

Preheat oven to 190°C/375°F/gas mark 5. Lightly grease a 23×33cm/9×13in baking tin and set aside.

In a food processor, or in a mixing bowl using a fork, blend oat bran, cocoa, and bicarbonate of soda. Transfer to a bowl.

In a small bowl combine milk, oil, and vanilla.

Whip egg whites until almost stiff. Slowly, about 3 tablespoons at a time, add the sugar to the whites and continue to beat until they are thick.

Stir the liquid ingredients into the dry ones; the batter will be crumbly. Stir one-quarter of the egg-white mixture into the oat-bran batter to lighten and moisten it, then add another quarter of the whites. Fold the last half of the egg whites into the lightened batter and spoon into the prepared baking tin. Bake for 30 minutes.

Prune and Date Bars

Makes 16 bars

While most baked goods are best straight out of the oven, these are better
if left to stand for a day. They keep well for up to a week, and are welcome
treats in a lunch bag at school or work.

FILLING
50g/2oz brown sugar
25g/1oz apple fibre
175g/6oz finely-chopped
    stoned prunes

75g/3oz finely-chopped stoned
    dates

DOUGH
100g/4oz oatmeal, **not quick-
    cooking kind**
100g/4oz oat bran
50g/2oz apple fibre
¼ teaspoon ground cinnamon
200g/7oz brown sugar

150g/5oz plain flour, sifted
    with ½ teaspoon baking
    powder
6 egg whites
4 tablespoons corn oil

Preheat oven to 180°C/350°F/gas mark 4. Lightly grease a
20cm/8in baking tin.

To make filling, combine brown sugar and 250ml/8fl oz water
in a small saucepan; bring to the boil. Stir in apple fibre, prunes,
and dates, and simmer 3 to 5 minutes; mixture should be thick.
Set aside.

In a large mixing bowl, combine oatmeal, oat-bran, apple fibre,
cinnamon, brown sugar, and flour. With a whisk or your hands,
combine ingredients until thoroughly mixed.

Add egg whites and oil. With your hands, squeeze ingredients
together; dough should just hold together and be quite crumbly.
If dough is too dry and some particles do not adhere, sprinkle a
tablespoon of water over the dough and mix again. Divide dough
in half.

Pat half of the dough into the prepared baking tin. With a
spatula, spread the prune-and-date filling over dough. Between
two pieces of greaseproof paper, roll the dough into a square the
size of your baking tin, and lay this dough over the filling, trying

to cover the entire surface. Bake for 35 to 40 minutes. Cool to room temperature before cutting.

Raspberry Fool

Makes 4 servings

A classic raspberry fool calls for puréed fruit blended into whipped cream. In this version we purée the fruit with apple fibre to thicken it and fold the purée into a meringue. You can make it especially festive by putting a few fresh raspberries on top and drizzling a bit of raspberry liqueur over it.

2 × 275g/10oz packets frozen raspberries in light syrup, thawed

20g/¾ oz apple fibre
3 egg whites
50g/2oz sugar

Purée frozen raspberries and their syrup in a food processor or blender. To eliminate the seeds, push the raspberries through a sieve, mashing down on the purée with a spoon. Discard the seeds.

Blend apple fibre into the raspberry purée and simmer over low heat for 3 minutes. Cool the mixture to room temperature, then chill. About 1 hour before serving, beat the egg whites until stiff, gradually adding the sugar. Fold into the raspberry purée and apple fibre. Spoon into 4 serving dishes or large wine glasses and chill for an hour.

Mocha Pudding

Makes 1 serving

You can make a single serving of this cholesterol-lowering pudding, or a batch to keep in the refrigerator. Use more or less cocoa and coffee to taste.

1 heaped teaspoon guar gum	**½ teaspoon instant coffee**
3 tablespoon sugar	**3 tablespoons skimmed milk**
2 tablespoons unsweetened cocoa	**½ teaspoon vanilla essence**

In a small saucepan mix together, with a wire whisk, guar gum, sugar, cocoa, and instant coffee. Whisk until well blended. Gradually beat in the skimmed milk, vanilla, and 175ml/6fl oz water. Mix until well blended and smooth.

Bring mixture to a slow boil, stirring constantly with a wooden spoon. Be sure to get into the corners of the pan, where the guar gum tends to settle and lump. Stir well so that the pudding is lump-free. When the mixture comes to a boil, remove from heat and cool to room temperature. Refrigerate for 3 hours at least or until well chilled.

Berry Pudding

Makes 2 servings

This pudding is good enough to serve to company. Be sure to tell your guests the added benefit you're giving them in terms of cholesterol lowering! Put a few pieces of fresh fruit on top for a stunning presentation.

3 heaped teaspoons guar gum
2 tablespoons sugar
275g/10oz packet frozen
  raspberries or strawberries,
  in light syrup, thawed

½ teaspoon vanilla
½ cup low-fat yogurt

In a blender or food processor, mix guar gum, sugar, raspberries and their syrup, vanilla, and yogurt. Blend thoroughly. (You can, if you wish, first pass this mixture through a strainer to remove the raspberry seeds.)

Transfer the mixture to a small saucepan and slowly bring to a boil, stirring constantly with a wooden spoon (be sure to get into the corners of the pan, where the guar gum tends to settle and lump). Stir well so that the pudding is lump-free. When the mixture comes to a boil, simmer for 2 minutes, then remove from the heat. Transfer mixture to 2 dishes and cool to room temperature. Refrigerate for 3 hours at least or until well chilled.

Indian Barley Pudding

Makes 6 to 8 servings

Barley has cholesterol-lowering ability and this pudding is a really delicious way to enjoy it. You can increase the soluble-fibre content of the dish by sprinkling rice bran on top.

200g/7oz barley, pearled or
   whole
350ml/12fl oz skimmed milk
4 tablespoons molasses
¼ teaspoon each powdered
   cloves, cinnamon, and
   nutmeg

2 tablespoons rum
4 egg whites
150g/5oz raisins

Preheat oven to 160°C/325°F/gas mark 3. Lightly grease a wide, shallow ovenproof glass or ceramic baking dish, about 23 × 33cm/ 9 × 13in and set aside.

In a large saucepan bring barley, milk, 1.15 litres/2 pints water, molasses, spices, and rum to the boil and simmer 3 minutes. Remove from heat and cool 10 minutes. In a small mixing bowl combine egg whites with raisins, and after 10 minutes, stir this into the barley-milk mixture. Pour the mixture into the prepared baking dish and bake for 1½ hours.

Serve warm or at room temperature.

Rice Pudding

Makes six 100g/4oz servings

Traditional rice pudding might taste good, but it contains virtually no fibre and is high in fat. Here we've added back the fibre in the form of either rice bran or apple fibre. Each will give the dish a distinctive flavour. Serve the pudding at room temperature, since rice tends to be tough when chilled.

450ml/¾ pint water
350ml/12fl oz skimmed milk
90g/3½ oz sugar
150g/5oz raisins
1 teaspoon vanilla essence or
* ½ teaspoon almond extract*

200g/7oz parboiled long-grain
* rice*
4-6 tablespoons finely ground
* rice bran or apple fibre*
Cinnamon or sliced
* strawberries*

In a medium-sized saucepan, bring skimmed milk, 450ml/¾ pint water, sugar, raisins, and vanilla to a slow boil. Gently, in a steady stream, add rice and stir a couple of times. Lower heat and simmer, partially covered, for 25 minutes, or until rice is very tender.

When rice is soft, stir in rice bran and cook for 1 minute more. Transfer rice pudding to a 750ml/1¼ pint dish or to six ramekins or glass pudding dishes.

Serve at room temperature garnished with a dusting of cinnamon or sliced fresh strawberries.

Fruit and Fibre Jelly

Makes 6 to 8 servings

Everyone has room for at least a light dessert to end a meal sweetly. This recipe fills that need perfectly. Have a few servings prepared in the fridge for when the snack craving hits later in the evening.

75g/3oz jelly, strawberry or   *3 egg whites*
  raspberry flavoured   *40g/1 ½ oz sugar*
25g/1oz apple fibre
225g/8oz tin apricots, drained
  and chopped

Dissolve jelly in 250ml/8fl oz boiling water and set aside.

In a small bowl dissolve apple fibre in 250ml/8fl oz warm water, then stir in cut-up fruit. Whisk dissolved jelly into fibre and fruit.

Whip egg whites until they form stiff peaks, then gradually beat in sugar. Fold this into jelly, fibre, and fruit.

Spoon into 6 or 8 glass or ceramic ramekins and chill for 3 hours.

Chocolate Milkshake

Makes 1 serving

Many people think they can't enjoy the flavour of chocolate when watching their cholesterol counts. The truth is that cocoa powder has no fat or cholesterol; it's only when cocoa powder gets mixed with butterfat to make chocolate that it becomes an artery clogger. This milkshake offers not only a chocolate fix but also a good dose of soluble fibre by way of the guar gum.

1 heaped teaspoon guar gum
*2 tablespoons unsweetened
  cocoa*

*2 tablespoons sugar
100ml/4fl oz skimmed milk,
  preferably chilled*

In a food processor or blender, combine guar gum, cocoa, and sugar; mix until well blended. In a measuring cup, combine skimmed milk and 3 tablespoons water. While blender or food processor is running, pour in the liquid and mix for about a minute or until thickened. Drink as it is or on ice.

Variations
To make a mocha shake, use 1 tablespoon cocoa and 1 teaspoon instant coffee.

To make a coffee shake, omit cocoa and use 1 to 1½ teaspoons instant coffee.

To make a vanilla shake, use 1 tablespoon vanilla essence.

Orange Guar

Makes 1 serving

When you're in the mood for a tasty fibre-packed drink, try this. You can get guar gum in major health-food stores, and one teaspoon has as much soluble fibre as an oat-bran muffin.

1 heaped teaspoon guar gum, preferably orange-flavoured
2 tablespoons sugar
2 tablespoons frozen orange-juice concentrate, thawed

1 teaspoon vanilla essence
100ml/4fl oz skimmed milk, preferably chilled

In a blender or food processor combine guar gum and sugar; mix until blended. In a measuring cup, mix orange-juice concentrate, vanilla, skimmed milk, and 3 tablespoons water. While blender or food processor is running, pour in the liquid. Mix for a minute or until thickened and well homogenized. Serve as it is or on ice.

Orange Guar Smoothie

Makes 1 serving

Treat yourself to this creamy orange whip. The guar gum adds soluble fibre as well as acting as a thickener.

2 heaped tablespoons frozen orange-juice concentrate
1 heaped teaspoon orange-flavoured guar gum

175ml/6fl oz natural low-fat yogurt
Sugar or sugar substitute to taste

Place all ingredients in a blender for a few seconds and enjoy.

Index

THE 8-WEEK CHOLESTEROL CURE

Robert E. Kowalski

The 2 million-copy-plus hardback bestseller

A safe, effective and revolutionary approach to lowering blood cholesterol that shows you how to:

★ Cut your risk of heart attack by more than half.

★ Limit the amount of cholesterol produced by your body.

★ Increase the amount of cholesterol eliminated by your body.

★ Raise the level of HDL ('the good cholesterol') in your blood.

★ Use special foods and vitamins that actually lower total blood cholesterol *without going hungry*.

★ Enjoy a variety of foods whether eating in or dining out.

★ Increase your chances for a long, healthy life.

'Readable, well documented and extremely practical in its approach . . . a cheerful and positive book that can be warmly recommended to anyone interested in lowering their own or other people's blood cholesterol levels.' *Cardiology in Practice*.

'Everyone who's ever been told by their doctor to lower their cholesterol will benefit.' - *Woman's Realm*.

CHOLESTEROL AND CHILDREN

Robert E. Kowalski

**The parent's guide to giving children
a future free of heart disease**

The build-up of cholesterol levels in the blood can begin in childhood, and studies of schoolchildren have shown that half of those tested have abnormal coronary arteries by the age of 15, and that the diets of about half the children from 10 to 15 contain levels of fat in excess of Department of Health recommendations.

Here is a programme specially designed for children based on Robert Kowalski's dramatic cholesterol lowering strategy outlined in *The 8-Week Cholesterol Cure*.

He shows how to modify your family's eating habits easily and happily, so that you can give your children the chance of a future free of heart disease. He also includes advice on helping your children cope with stress and stay physically fit, in an age when children are less active, more overweight and more highly stressed than ever before.